MY YEARS AT THE AUSTRIAN COURT
: BY NELLIE RYAN :
WITH SIXTEEN ILLUSTRATIONS

LONDON: JOHN LANE, THE BODLEY HEAD
NEW YORK: JOHN LANE COMPANY MCMXV

To Miss Nellie Ryan with sincere thanks from Archduke Charles Stephen

Zywiec Castle 15th Sept..

ARCHDUKE KARL STEFAN

DEDICATED TO
THE YOUNGEST DAUGHTER
OF THE EMPRESS

PREFACE

SINCE the writing of this volume of reminiscences, Warsaw, the capital of Russian Poland, has been captured by Austro-German forces and the Russian armies have been forced to evacuate Galicia.

Rumour now has it that Poland is to be united under a king once more, and that Archduke Karl Stefan of Austria is to be offered the throne.

I spent many months at the Archduke's castle in Galicia, and can affirm that the Poles in that neighbourhood have much affection and esteem for the kindly Archduke and his family. Two of his daughters, Archduchesses Renata and Mechtildis, are married to distinguished members of the Polish nobility, the first to Prince Jerome Radziwill, and the second to Prince Olgierd Czartoryski. That the crown should be offered to Karl Stefan comes as a surprise to me, because it was generally understood, when I was in Galicia, that if Poland had a king again, the choice would fall on Prince Jerome Radziwill.

But, in these days of world-upheavals, old points of view and present speculations are of little value, and it would be indeed rash to attempt to forecast the immediate future of Poland. This little book will show, if further need be, the characteristics of Archduke Karl Stefan that would make him an acceptable ruler of that country.

August, 1915

CONTENTS

CONTENTS

x

ILLUSTRATIONS

MY YEARS AT THE
AUSTRIAN COURT

B

MY YEARS AT THE : AUSTRIAN COURT :

CHAPTER I

IS THE IMPERIAL HOUSE OF AUSTRIA MAD?

IT has been written that the Emperor of Austria is most unlucky in his family circle, because the shadow of madness dogs the footsteps of the Hapsburgs, and there is hardly any branch of the family which does not possess some insane, epileptic or vicious member.

As I spent some delightful years at the Court of Vienna, and personally knew many of these so-called degenerate Hapsburgs, it is my intention to write of those whom I always found extremely clever and interesting, and by no means mad. If at this great European crisis we compare the two Kaisers, around whom the nations of the world are fighting, we find two men of totally different characters: William II, the German Emperor, who forced this terrible war—a madman if ever a ruler lived—and Franz Josef, the Emperor of Austria, peace-loving, sad and weary, on whom this war was forced.

Yet how often the word " mad " is associated with the old Austrian Emperor and his family ! Would it not be nearer the truth if some of these utterly false rumours and insinuations were directed to the other ruler—to the man who has plunged the whole world into ruin and disaster ?

During the years I spent in Austria, whether it was from his near relatives at Court or from amongst the people of the land, I heard nothing but words of love, respect and reverence for the aged monarch, who was wont to mingle amongst his people in a simple and unostentatious manner, and who was so renowned for his kindness and generosity to the poor.

The German Emperor never moves out unless great and extravagant preparation is made : a herald must even be sent to proclaim, in loud and noisy tones, that His Imperial Majesty is passing into the next street. In his palaces his very menials are sometimes restricted in their food allowance. It is notorious his love of inviting himself—perhaps with half an hour's notice, or even less—to breakfast or dinner at the Casino of some regiment, or to the house of a noble or an official of Berlin, according to the whim of the moment. The host, whoever he may be, knows only too well that His Majesty expects the menu to be of the highest grade, the wines of the very choicest.

Furthermore, at such events as birthdays, house parties, and visits paid to the hunting boxes of friends, whom the Emperor honours with his costly presence, nothing is too good that money can buy. His Majesty expects the greatest caterers of Paris or Berlin to send the most expensive delicacies of the season, and a special *chef* must be engaged from some world-famed restaurant.

As the Kaiser never travels with fewer than twenty attendants and their servants, the cost of even a so-called impromptu visit is stupendous, and the preparation and anxiety attending these all too frequent surprise visits call for some kind of appreciation and thanks.

The Kaiser takes it all as a matter of course, merely remarking on leaving that it pleases him to feel he is always free to visit his people, without inflicting any trouble or expense upon them.

His actions on all occasions show to the world his hard-heartedness, ill-temper and lack of mental balance.

During the Emperor Franz Josef's reign there have been untold sorrows and tragedies; yet now, in his eighty-fifth year, his mind is as clear and alert as ever, and beyond some few follies and mistakes of early youth no acts of cruelty, madness or egotism can be attributed to him.

He has been, and is still the most really beloved ruler in the world; and is always ready to help his poorer subjects.

He was born in 1830 at the beautiful palace at Schönbrunn, and was the son of Archduke Franz Karl and Archduchess Sophia. The throne of Austria loomed above him from his birth; and, throughout his boyhood, he was continually reminded of his great future; whilst other boys played and made merry, Franz Josef was listening to lectures, learning many languages, and being instructed in the complications of statecraft.

As he was to rule over a country where a dozen languages and dialects were spoken, the task was of the most difficult, and he had no natural talent for speaking Italian, Hungarian, Czech, Polish, Croatian and Serbian. But he was made to learn by a haughty, fierce and ambitious mother, who was responsible for the spoiling of his boyhood, and the wrecking of his early married life.

His difficulties in respect to languages have had no grave results, except in regard to his vast dominions in Hungary, where it has been a lasting grievance with the Hungarian people that their sovereign has never really mastered their beloved language, and this especially in the early days of his reign, when the estrangement between Austria and Hungary was so much more marked than it is now.

On several occasions, both at official and private audiences, the difficulty of expressing himself easily and fluently has left a hostile feeling amongst the Hungarians, even to this day.

The early years of Franz Josef were almost

without affection, and he seems to have received very few of the little loving-kindnesses that vary a dull and monotonous boyhood.

Soon after his twelfth birthday, his tyrannical and unscrupulous mother seems to have left him almost entirely under the tutorship of Count Bombelles, who, from all one hears in Vienna, had the worst possible influence over the early years of Franz Josef, and of many other members of the Austrian Court. A loathsome hypocrite, with no ideas of right and wrong, this tutor of Franz Josef was certainly the worst possible guide for the early manhood of a young Emperor.

If one remembers the state of affairs in Austria, when, at the age of eighteen, Franz Josef ascended the throne, and indeed many of the years to follow, one cannot help marvelling at the skill with which he tackled the difficulties, first of Vienna itself, then Bohemia, Italy and Hungary.

The dissensions in the latter country lasted long, because the Hungarians did not want to be ruled by Austria, in fact they did not regard Franz Josef as their King until he had been crowned at their capital.

Then, with many political troubles raging, disliked by the Hungarians from the early part of his reign, and just after his life was attempted—which he bravely let pass unheeded —he made himself a little more popular by his romantic marriage with his sixteen-year-old cousin Elizabeth, daughter of Duke Maximilian of Bavaria. She was the most beautiful princess in the world, literally idolised by all the Bavarian people, and her picture, even to-day, is seen in many a peasant's cottage, being looked upon by them as the portrait of a saint.

The marriage was neither completely happy nor wholly successful, but the mischief was wrought at the beginning by the Emperor's mother—in this case a truly unpleasant and most unscrupulous woman.

Besides the mother-in-law—Archduchess Sophia—one must not forget to mention her followers, her friends, and the spies she set around to watch, and magnify the doings and sayings of this royal couple, who undoubtedly were very much in love with each other, and quite prepared to be thoroughly happy.

Franz Josef was brave, gracious and always

most desirous to make everything as pleasant as possible for every one; and his beautiful bride, who had Hungarian blood in her veins, at once captivated that country, and all its people.

Fate, however, seems to have stepped in. The young Empress found no friend at Court, and misunderstandings wrecked what should have been a romantic and beautiful marriage.

Sorrows and tragedies fell thick and fast, but notwithstanding it all, and in spite of what one reads and hears, there were many moments of real happiness for those two. When the bitter and overwhelming news reached Franz Josef that his beautiful and beloved wife had been assassinated, the words which he let fall to those few around him, " My God! the world will never know what she was to me," clearly point out, what very few realise, that Franz Josef really loved his wife.

The Emperor contributed greatly to his popularity by his passion for sports. He was a marvellous shot, and was frequently to be met, in the wilds of the mountains and in the shadow of the great forests, attired simply in the regulation Austrian shooting costume—

very short leather knickerbockers, a little short jacket, heavily nailed boots, and the charming Tyrolese hat.

But, amidst all his many sports, Franz Josef never failed to take long periodical journeys to visit the Empress during her sojourn in distant places. On the many occasions when she was absent from the various Court functions and ceremonies, he was never known to complain aloud, but went about wearing always that look of imperturbable calm and patience to which the world has long since become accustomed.

And there were so many other troubles, besides those of his own family, that he has had to face during the whole of his long reign. Italy has always been a difficulty, and Germany a dark shadow; Hungary has risen, but has been practically conquered, as it were, and subdued by his marriage, and by his journeying to the capital to be crowned.

Besides these countries, there have been Russia, France and many others that have kept Franz Josef always on the edge of war; and of late years that race of people so near at hand, the Serbians, men fierce and patriotic, whose antagonism to Austrian designs gradually increased until, in 1914, the crisis came when Austria's future Emperor was killed on Serbian soil.

Yes, most surely Franz Josef has lived a life, the equal of which no Emperor or King for hundreds of years has ever experienced.

But no madness or moments of insanity can be traced to Austria's wonderful old monarch, in spite of all the sorrows and tragedies, and in spite of all the insinuations and stories one has been so accustomed to hear.

Since Elizabeth's death, he has led the simplest of lives, whether it has been at the great Hofburg in Vienna, at Schönbrunn, the beautiful palace and park on the outskirts of Vienna, or at Ischl, the summer residence, which is but a picturesque and quite simple villa.

The Emperor for many years has slept on a simple camp bed, and rises each morning about five o'clock. Until this last year a certain amount of state business was transacted before breakfast, which the Emperor was accustomed to take about half-past seven. This early breakfast merely consists of coffee, rolls and butter; after which, when in good health, the Emperor takes a short walk, and is very soon back at his desk.

At ten o'clock two or three slices of sausage and bread are served; the great post is then brought in, and various audiences are granted, often to his poorer subjects.

The smaller meals are always served in the private study of the Emperor, and the lunch, which takes place at half-past twelve or one o'clock, consists of soup, fish, vegetables, a light sweet, fruit and coffee, with, generally, a small glass of wine.

The dinner at night is a still lighter meal, very often consisting of a roll, a thin slice of ham and a small glass of wine or beer. By nine o'clock Franz Josef of Austria retires to rest; and most surely to this regular, moderate life must be attributed his very long reign and wonderful health.

To the lunch only, which is served in the large dining hall, a guest or two may be bidden. There is still solemn and simple grandeur, where the Empress is no more, and flowers are never seen; but sometimes Franz Josef's mind goes back to the old days of glory, and he sees again the great doors gliding back, and he himself, leading the once beautiful Empress, enters, followed by the brilliant Court.

And to-day! How inexpressibly sad, and much more tragic than anything that has gone before, must be the thoughts that surge through the mind of the aged Emperor after nearly one long year of terrible fighting and bloodshed.

To think that after all the many sorrows and calamities which have fallen to his lot, this most inhuman war, now raging throughout Europe, should blight his last few hours. One must pity him and be sorry for him in these closing days of a long and hitherto prosperous reign.

For some time quite recently he has been at death's door, prostrate with horror and grief, at the terrible losses his beloved country has undergone, and at the brutalities committed by his German Allies.

But by a superhuman effort he has crawled from his bed of sickness and once again taken up his accustomed position. There one may picture him sitting at his favourite desk, pen in hand, granting innumerable audiences, ready to help, suggest, and to act, trying in vain to bring about peace; and one may imagine this splendid old Emperor, shutting his eyes to the fact, refusing to believe that he is being made to witness the beginning of the downfall of Austria.   Even this, the greatest tragedy of all, in his venerable old age, has not been spared Franz Josef.

CHAPTER II

THE EMPRESS ELIZABETH

EVERY one knows how the Emperor Franz Josef, when he arrived at Possenhofen to celebrate his engagement to Helene, the eldest daughter of Duke Maximilian and Princess Ludovica of Bavaria, accidentally met the little Elizabeth in one of the avenues of the park, and fell straightway in love, and how he insisted upon her joining in the festivities, much to the annoyance of her parents and sisters.

" I shall marry no one but the little Elizabeth," said the young Emperor the next morning, when he demanded the hand of this particular Princess; and he was for the moment starting off for his own estates, when the old Duke reluctantly gave his consent.

After a few weeks they were married, and the union of this young and handsome couple would have been completely happy had it not been

16

THE EMPEROR AND EMPRESS OF AUSTRIA

for the inevitable mother-in-law, who has wrecked the early lives of so many of our reigning sovereigns. Archduchess Sophia cared for nobody, or nothing, as long as she continued to reign supreme ; and she hated, at first sight, the beautiful and saint-like Elizabeth.

The whole Court, from the first, followed the example of Archduchess Sophia, and seized every opportunity to vex, humiliate and wound the girl-wife.

Only a few moments after their return to the Hofburg from a short trip through Bohemia and Moravia, the Empress wished to speak to Franz Josef in his own apartments. At the entrance, which was guarded by several gentle-men-in-waiting, she was respectfully asked what message could be delivered to His Majesty.

" Pray stand aside," said the young Empress haughtily, " I am about to speak to His Majesty myself."

" Your Imperial Majesty must pardon my reminding Your Imperial Majesty that no one passes into the presence of His Imperial Majesty without permission," said the attendant with a low and courtly bow, whilst around stood several impassive figures.

c

In vain the young Empress demanded and protested. She was compelled to wait, and be announced like a stranger ; and when at length she swept into her husband's presence, expecting to have this matter put right, she was amazed to find that, although the Emperor laughingly tried to soothe her wounded feelings, he made her firmly understand that even between husband and wife etiquette at the Viennese Court must always be observed.

And this etiquette rose up against her at every corner—all her wishes, her freedom and her amusements were frustrated.

She was devoted to riding and walking ; but neither was considered correct for an Empress, she was always told by Archduchess Sophia.

When she found that there was never a moment during the day that she could see her husband alone, too miserable to make complaints, and too young to assert her own rights, gradually Elizabeth's feelings dried up within her, and she complained no more.

And the Emperor ? He was still passionately in love with her perfect beauty, but he had no time to study Elizabeth's peculiar nature. Affairs of state, sport, the continual

round of gaieties, and the intriguing and insinuations of his mother, soon began to force
these two apart, and only too soon he fell into
the grievous fault of believing his wife, so lovely,
pure and innocent, a thing apart. She was for
him too inexperienced and too indifferent.

And then it is impossible to ignore the fact
that the Emperor indulged in many a flirtation.
Sometimes, too, they were of so serious a
nature that it was not at all likely they could
go unheeded by Elizabeth, who was utterly
unable to understand or excuse such lapses
from her own pure and lofty ideals.

Many of these affairs had been grossly
exaggerated, and by the time they reached her
unwilling ears were very often entirely false;
but one has to admit there was a certain amount
of truth in some of them.

There is the story of his attentions to the
beautiful, but unscrupulous Countess, forced
upon him at a Court ball by Archduchess
Sophia, nearly a year after his marriage, which
caused the young Empress her first bitter
awakening. Matters, too, were made ten times
worse when the news was conveyed to her, a
few days later, that the fascinating lady had

been appointed maid of honour to her mother-in-law.

After sleepless nights of nérvous exhaustion, when she had spent hours of trepidation trying to reason herself into believing it must all be her own imagination, or a great and ghastly mistake, she at length made up her mind to unburden her heart to her mother, Archduchess Ludovica, sister of Archduchess Sophia. Instead of kind and loving words of encouragement and counsel, she coldly pointed out to her now thoroughly miserable daughter that she was complaining unnecessarily and her imagination had taken possession of her senses.

" Is it not possible for you to be content with being Empress of Austria, surrounded by every luxury and attention ? It is time indeed you grew accustomed to your great position. It is no good putting on the face of a martyr or a saint. Look about you, and try to console yourself as others do."

Some days later, Elizabeth noticed that on all occasions a cavalier was being forced upon her. He was a smart young officer, and a great rider, whose amiability and kindness very soon won him a place in the heart of the unsuspicious

Empress. Archduchess Sophia, in arranging the riding parties and other expeditions, managed matters so skilfully that soon the Empress began to lose a little of her reserve, and to treat her attendant cavalier with friendly confidence.

For a brief space of time, Elizabeth really began to take interest in life again. Gossip began to connect the name of the handsome young officer with that of the Empress. They danced and rode much together, and one night at Schönbrunn towards the end of a brilliant ball, when as usual her matchless beauty reigned supreme, they found themselves in the great palm court of the palace.

The Empress that night wore an exquisite dress of dazzling white, with a single row of pearls reaching to the hem of her satin gown. Her glorious chestnut hair was braided high up on her shapely head ; and she was, to all those who saw her that memorable night, a dream of youth and beauty. She seemed to have flung away her fears and recent unhappiness, and was talking away in her bewitching voice, utterly unconscious of the torrent of emotion she was rousing in the man at her side.

" Elizabeth, listen to me. I love you, and you must know it," he broke forth, casting himself on his knees, and speaking in a broken and trembling voice.

Seizing hold of her hands, he forced her to listen to his passionate declaration of love.

" Dearest, my beloved Empress, do not send me away. Only let me be your slave ; give me just one small corner in your heart so that you can know there is at least one man at this wretched Court who would willingly die for you—I ask nothing more."

" Sir, you forget yourself ! " haughtily exclaimed the Empress, wrenching herself free. " How can you speak of love to me—I, who love my husband ? " And almost choking with fury she went on, " Do you take me for one of the many so-called ladies of this Court ? No one has ever presumed to insult *me* before. Go, and leave me."

In vain the man tried to explain, to apologise. Seeing he did not go, Elizabeth walked abruptly from the palm court, and summoning one of her ladies repaired at once to her private apartments.

Before her twenty-first birthday, the Empress

gave birth to her third child, a son and heir.
Her first little girl had died, and the second,
Gisela, had been taken from her care by her
mother-in-law.

"Now," said the proud Empress, "every one
will be so pleased with me, surely I shall be
allowed to keep my boy."

But in this she was mistaken. Although the
Emperor had promised her she should personally
superintend the bringing up of the little Rudolph,
the Archduchess Sophia again interfered, and
said it was not practicable or possible that the
heir of so vast an Empire should be under the
direct control of so young a mother. Once more
her child was carried off to nurseries in a far-
away part of the palace, and jealously guarded
by attendants chosen by the Archduchess herself.

It is impossible to describe the agony of
despair of this royal but helpless mother : she
had hoped to begin life afresh from the day of
her son's birth. But no—the cruelty of the
mother-in-law robbed her of her son's care, and
her husband's heart had already been stolen
from her. For a year or two, she walked through
life with eyes and ears closed, haughty, cold and
proud to all around her.

The flirtations of the Emperor continued, until, at last, a very unfortunate adventure brought matters to a climax and broke the last restraint upon her indignation. This happened when the actress Frau Roll, of no particular fame, except for her marvellous beauty and figure, made her appearance at the principal theatre in Vienna, and was afterwards to be seen staying in the neighbourhood of Ischl, when the Court was in residence there. The Empress, when the scandalous tales were brought to her notice, succeeded in getting the Emperor to banish the fair lady from Ischl by threatening to leave the Court herself unless this was done.

No sooner was this adventure over, than we hear of the Emperor's shooting parties becoming so attractive that he remained for several days at his shooting-box, in the forest not far from Vienna. The story reached the poor distracted Empress of the attractive gamekeeper's daughter, who was to be found in the neighbourhood of this particular shooting-box.

Summoning one of her faithful attendants, she bade her quickly prepare for an unexpected journey. When all was ready, taking only a hired conveyance, they cautiously left the palace, drove to the station, and took train for the coast, unseen by a soul.

At Trieste they boarded her own yacht, and set sail down the Adriatic.

One has no conception of the consternation and alarm created by this flight, or the torrent of wrath flung at her head for daring to take matters in her own hand, and for so recklessly breaking the chain of convention.

The repentant, and nearly demented Emperor went off himself at once, in an unsuccessful pursuit. As soon as the Empress learnt of this, the direction of the yacht was changed, and they set sail for other lands and the ocean beyond.

The Emperor was forced to return to Vienna, a sadder and an older man—so filled with bitter shame and regret that to this day he is a changed man.

And so the months rolled on, and the gay Court of Vienna missed the beautiful figure of its lost Empress. Archduchess Sophia reigned supreme, but somehow, not quite as she wished —Elizabeth had left her mark, and was missed by many.

Incognita, Elizabeth cruised in many waters, from Norway down to the Mediterranean, and made exhaustive studies of the coasts of Greece and Africa, until she found a spot on the coast of Algeria where she took possession of a quaint old mansion, in which she tried her utmost to forget her misery by deep study and much physical exercise.

Now that the Empress had time to ponder and reflect, she tried very earnestly to make herself forgive her husband's many failings. Elizabeth tried to argue that because of his exalted position, and his extraordinary personal charm, she must try to remember that he was surrounded by untold temptations, and pursued by countless flatterers.

A very long time passed by before this sad and lamentable estrangement came to an end —and although during this period, for state and political reasons, the Empress was forced to appear in public on special occasions, as soon as these irksome duties were accomplished she left Vienna and lived her own secluded life.

Many arguments were brought forward by influential people. The health of the little Rudolph, and her husband's genuine and deep sorrow, finally made her see where her duty lay.

The home-coming of the Empress was at first not an easy task. Naturally Rudolph, now about six years of age, was indifferent to his mother, and utterly spoilt by his grandmother. He was a very nervous and excitable child, and his every whim had been gratified.

Very soon, however, her physical charm, and her loving patience influenced the little boy to a remarkable degree; and it was not very long before Elizabeth had completely gained his love.

By the time he was ten years old, the Crown Prince Rudolph was a gay, fascinating boy, adored by all, and his shyness of his beautiful mother had entirely disappeared.

CHAPTER III

THE JOYS AND SORROWS OF AN EMPRESS

ARCHDUCHESS VALÉRIE was born in 1868 ; and for a time some little gleams of happiness stole into the life of the Empress, with her two little daughters and the little Crown Prince.

She was of great comfort to Franz Josef, who about this time received the terrible news of the assassination of his brother, the Emperor Maximilian of Mexico.

All who noticed Elizabeth's untiring sympathy, and devotion to the Emperor at this period, were much impressed by it ; and it seemed as though she was doing her utmost to make up for their long separation.

Innumerable too were the charities started by her, in and around Vienna ; and the lasting good she worked is one of the beautiful memories she has left behind her for the Emperor and Vienna.

Her little daughter Valérie grew to be a real companion to her. She inherited all her mother's love of sport and outdoor life, and rode almost as well as the Empress.

I have scarcely mentioned the extraordinary prowess of the Empress as a horsewoman. Her fame is world-renowned, and one constantly hears that there never has been a rider with whom she can be compared; she rode any horse, and with her marvellous hypnotic power she could always tame the wildest.

The marriage of her daughter Valérie to Archduke Franz Salvator was a great popular event; she was the constant reminder to her parents of their reconciliation, and greatly beloved by all the people. The marriage is a very happy one; although again in the recent records which have been lately published a very different tale is often told. On my last visit to Vienna, she came several times to visit Archduchess Maria Theresa, and I recall her great charm, and kindliness of manner.

When I was first presented to her at the Palais Friedrich by Archduchess Maria Theresa, I remember she said how much she always admired the English, and everything that was

English, and how much she regretted her inability to converse as fluently as she wished.

To this day she continues to follow in her mother's footsteps by her unceasing devotion to the poor.

In the case of the Empress, her untiring charities, and the wonderful methods she employed in rescuing numerous families from suffering and want, helped to keep her mind occupied to a certain extent. Early morning, or late at night, at all odd times in the day, whether in town or country, she would steal out of the palace accompanied only by one faithful attendant. She went into the poorest and darkest hovels, and no one ever knew that the kind, gentle lady was the same haughty and indifferent Empress who was so misjudged by many of her subjects.

When the time came for the marriage of the Crown Prince, I think Elizabeth went through agonies of apprehension.

In the endless discussions of the possible bride—and there was at that time a great lack of eligible princesses—her anxiety and nervousness for her dearly loved and only son were intense. When it was finally decided Rudolph should marry Stéphanie, daughter of the late King of the Belgians and Archduchess Marie Henriette, herself daughter of Archduke Joseph, the Empress bitterly opposed the marriage. She never liked King Leopold, and still less his consort ; and she felt convinced, from all she had heard of the Princess Stéphanie, that she could not possibly make an ideal wife for her son, who possessed ideas and tastes utterly different from those of the Belgian Princess. All through the short engagement, Elizabeth was terribly despondent, and filled with a persistent presentiment of the many deplorable tragedies and miseries that the marriage eventually brought about.

But the wedding took place, as we know so well, amidst enormous enthusiasm and excitement. The Crown Prince was adored by rich and poor, and he was extraordinarily popular ; for days beforehand people flocked into Vienna from far and wide, anxious to see as much as possible. Certainly the thousands who lined the roads from the palace to the Prater, on the day when the various Royalties drove in a gorgeous procession, witnessed one of the most magnificent sights.

There were between fifty and sixty state carriages; and, besides the Emperor and Empress, the King and Queen of the Belgians, the Crown Prince and his bride, Empress Frederick, King Edward and the German Emperor, there were many other foreign Royalties and distinguished visitors in this glittering procession. This was arranged by the ever-thoughtful Emperor, so that the great populace should have every opportunity of cheering their Prince and wishing him God-speed.

From the very beginning the marriage was unsatisfactory. Stéphanie was worldly, frivolous and very bad-tempered; and dissensions and quarrels occurred from an early date. She was utterly unsuited to be the wife of such a man as Rudolph. She had no sympathy with his love of literature and writing, and she heaped reproaches on him when he left her for the hunt, and other outdoor sport, of which he was extremely fond.

When their little daughter Elizabeth was born, matters became even worse; and Rudolph lost all patience. Then it was that he bought the shooting-box at Mayerling, where he spent a great part of his time, trying to forget his matrimonial troubles in scientific and literary pursuits, in hunting, in beautifying this retreat with all the trophies of the hunt, and in long hours in the world of music and painting.

The Empress was nearly heart-broken, and did all she could to smooth matters between the ill-assorted pair. Unfortunately, there was a set of people bribed by Stéphanie and her followers to watch every movement of the Crown Prince, and they were not very truthful in their reports. All sorts of stories and rumours were brought to the Crown Princess, reports that were utterly false; and her increasing anger at her husband's supposed unfaithfulness and ill-treatment brought matters to such a crisis that the Royal couple never met except in public.

But, as a matter of fact, Rudolph had never been in love. He never favoured the society of womenfolk, as reports suggest; although it is true that he got himself mixed up in various political intrigues.

When at the great Polish ball, in 1887, he met and straightway fell in love with the beautiful Baroness Marie Vetsera, then indeed his enemies had food for talk. Rudolph, by

D

this time, had become so reckless and so indifferent that he seems to have thrown prudence
to the winds. He danced with her repeatedly,
paying her marked attention ; and every day,
somewhere and somehow, they contrived to
see each other.

At last the Crown Prince determined to apply
to the Pope for a divorce, and he seems to have
confided in Duke Philip of Coburg, who was
the husband of Stéphanie's sister, Louise.

Philip was amazed and stupefied at the
tidings of his brother-in-law, and he omitted to
keep his promise. He told the state of affairs
to Archduke Franz Ferdinand, who was even
more shocked and horrified, and, being a highly
religious man, went straightway to the priest.
So, in this roundabout way, a letter reached
the Pope, putting the whole matter before him.

Immediately upon the receipt of this letter,
the Pope sent a special messenger to the
Emperor Franz Josef. One can imagine the
consternation and grief of the Emperor, who
already had some idea of the matrimonial rela-
tions of his son and daughter-in-law, but had
absolutely no warning that matters had taken
so disastrous a turn.

On January 29th, 1889, took place that terrible interview between the Emperor and his son, of which so much has been written, and so little is actually known.

Rudolph was hastily summoned by the Emperor, and was solemnly ushered into his presence, with no warning that the terrible state of his affairs had reached the Emperor's ears. Directly he saw, standing there, in his father's private study, the messenger from the Holy Father, the Crown Prince went white to the lips, and prepared for the worst. The Empress, at the same time, had been sent for, and entered the room almost at the same moment as her son.

He came forward as she entered, and kissed her hand, but between those two, each suffering for the other, no word could be passed.

.   .   .   .   .

Rudolph left the Hofburg a changed and broken-hearted man. But he gave his word to his sorrowing father that for a time at least he would give up Marie Vetsera.

He drove to Mayerling. There he wrote her a long letter, in which he said that, for some days they must not meet. The letter was taken by his faithful and devoted servant Bratfisch.

Marie Vetsera meanwhile had received a special messenger from the Emperor, who conveyed to her the Royal command that within twenty-four hours she should marry a certain nobleman. She obeyed neither the Emperor nor his son—but drove at once to Mayerling.

In the early morning, as all the world knows, Count Hoyos and the Prince of Coburg, who were staying at Mayerling for some shooting, were hastily called up by Bratfisch, who was alarmed because his master's door was locked, and he could obtain no answer to his repeated knocking. Becoming still more anxious and alarmed, they decided to burst open the door of the Prince's apartment, where they found the terrible sight of the Crown Prince shot through the head, and Marie Vetsera horribly disfigured.

The awful news was carried to the Empress by Count Hoyos, and it was she who went to break the horrible tidings to the Emperor.

The grief of these sorrowing parents was indescribable ; and the impression caused by the awful news throughout Vienna was pitiful. All kinds of stories and rumours were abroad, and much mystery was caused by several varied reports which were allowed to be published in the papers.

The whole dreadful business was hushed up in a wonderfully short space of time ; but from proofs brought to the Empress it seems quite certain that murder, not suicide, was the cause of the death of the Crown Prince.

For a long time the Empress fell into a strange unnatural calm, and would have given way entirely, if she had not been roused back to life, as it were, by the remembrance of the little Caroline, who seems to have been her one solace in life, and of whose extraordinary life I will speak later.

Certainly, from the time of the Crown Prince's tragic and terrible death until her own sad end in 1898, the Empress's health gave great cause for anxiety to those around her ; and it became necessary to try various cures and baths, and to travel very often to warmer climes. But it is not in the least true that she never smiled again after her beloved son's death, or that she refused to take any interest in life.

As for her love of travelling and change of
scene being called a mania, or a phase of madness, one might as well call " mad " the majority
of the well-to-do English and Americans who,
having plenty of leisure and money, think
nothing of spending five or six weeks at the
Winter Sports in Switzerland, moving on to
the South of France and Egypt for the next
month or so, rattling through a London season,
with half a dozen week-ends in Paris, and doing
a cure in July and August at Carlsbad or Marien-
bad. After which they are off to Scotland for
September and part of October ; then ready to
start for a " short " trip to India or China, to
escape the English Winter ; and are back again
in January for the Winter Sports, and the next
year's programme !

It is nothing ; it is not even criticised, and
yet all the world seems to wish to find some
excuse for talking of the mad Empress of
Austria, because she found a certain amount
of pleasure in change of scene and climate.

The Empress was neither mad nor even
always melancholy or sad. She was a woman
who was never heard to say or do an unkind
thing ; but she possessed a great horror of the

shams and narrow conventions practised by all those around her.

She was generous and warm-hearted to a degree, and often showed a merry, laughing side to the very few whom she loved and trusted. And above all, she had a great artistic soul, which yearned for a beautiful life, surrounded always by things beautiful.

CHAPTER IV

CAROLINE, YOUNGEST DAUGHTER OF
THE EMPRESS

THE Empress of Austria's determination that her fifth-born child, Caroline, should be brought up away from the Court, and in apparent obscurity, so that she could help to form the mind of at least one of her children, gives us yet another instance of a Wittelbach's resolution of character and strong will power.

This trait of the Empress lay hidden for many years ; and it was only on rare occasions that those around her realised that beneath her proud reserve, and apparent indifference, a great individuality was thirsting to live.

As one by one her children were taken from her, and made to live under the rigid etiquette of the Viennese Court, the extraordinary scheme unfolded itself in her mind, that Caroline

40

should be brought up away from the Court, and in entirely different surroundings.

In the year 1882 the Empress spent several months in Normandy, travelling about under the name of the Countess Hohenembs. News reached Vienna that the Empress had met with an accident whilst riding, and was laid up at the Château Sassetot, Petites Dalles. The Emperor visited her there occasionally, travelling incognito, and in this little corner of Normandy a fifth child was born.

Great secrecy was maintained, and to Professor Braun, the faithful friend and physician of the Empress, was given the difficult task of finding some kindly and reliable family with whom the Imperial child could be placed.

For the first few years Caroline was brought up as the daughter of an Austrian lady and her husband, people of good position, but not in the highest aristocratic circle of Viennese society. They lived in a delightful flat in the Opernring, Vienna, on the next floor to that occupied by the *costumier* of the Empress, so that it was without difficulty or suspicion that flying visits could be made to the little Archduchess in disguise.

Everything was done that could be to make the early years of the child's life happy, and it was not until the age of six years—when for the first time Caroline stayed under the same roof as her mother, at the Château of Lainz, outside Vienna—that the Empress explained to her little daughter that, instead of calling her " Aunt Elly " as she had hitherto done, she must call her " mother."

Soon after this flying visit Caroline was installed in a small house in Lainz, still under the superintendence of her guardians, but with the addition of new governesses and other attendants. From this time a very strict regime was enforced, and the course of study arranged was both wide and systematic. Until the age of nine, the life of the little Archduchess was sometimes very lonely and monotonous, with only occasional visits from the beautiful mother who travelled about so much.

When she was about ten, Caroline learnt that her mother was the Empress, and why it was she was kept hidden away from the Court. It took a very long time for her to grasp that she was a real Princess, and that it was her mother's wish she should grow up into a simple loving Princess amongst ordinary everyday folk.

About the year 1892, the Empress thought it advisable to put her little daughter under more efficient care than the guardians found by Professor Braun, who, though kind and loving, were not able to devote sufficient time and care to the difficult upbringing of a Princess in disguise.

To Frau von Friese was given this difficult task, though, to keep up the appearance of still being their daughter, several times a week visits were paid by Caroline to her old guardians.

It is generally supposed that most of the servants of the little Archduchess, who had been with her from her birth, had their suspicions as to her identity, but they were all too well paid to risk gossiping with the outside world.

With occasional visits to her Imperial mother, at Ischl, Langbath Lakes, and Venice, the time passed quite uneventfully until October, 1893, when Archduchess Caroline was sent to a day school in Vienna, with the idea of broadening her education, and giving her the opportunity of social intercourse with girls of her own age.

This plan gave great happiness to the Archduchess, and she gave herself up to hard study. She scarcely saw the Empress until the following spring, when she had the great joy of spending some weeks, under the care of Frau von Friese, in the South of France, actually staying in the same hotel as her Imperial mother.

As Frau von Friese was known to be an acquaintance of the Empress's of some years' standing, this arrangement passed off very happily for every one, and I believe many amusing anecdotes could be recorded of the walks taken together quite openly in that joyous sunny south.

How often has it been recorded that the Empress never smiled again after the murder of the Crown Prince? True, her heart was often bowed down with sorrow at her son's loss, but I have it on the authority of this youngest daughter—whom I know personally —that many hours of real happiness and much merriment were spent by these two in this romantic concealment, and that as Caroline grew up, although the Empress soon wearied of the company of all those around her, no hour was ever too long or tedious spent with the child brought up as she herself had desired and planned.

Up to the age of fifteen, although Caroline made many friends at the school, few visits were made by her to their houses. Many of the girls she would meet from time to time at her guardians' house in Vienna, and at the little parties that her foster-sister would arrange.

From this time onwards, little impromptu dances were given, and it was soon found that Caroline inherited her mother's great gift. Many pleasant and delightful hours were arranged by Frau von Friese, who seems to have been an able, conscientious companion, never once abusing her great trust, and giving up her whole time to the care of her young charge.

During this time, and until her terrible death, the Empress's health suffered considerably, and she was able to see her beloved daughter less than ever. Fourteen months before that fatal day, she was staying in Switzerland at the same hotel, and Caroline spent some little time with her.

Whilst there, reference was made to the time when Caroline would be grown-up enough to occupy her rightful position, and the Empress expressed her longing for that moment, after which there would be no more partings between these two who understood and loved each other so thoroughly. She said that the Emperor had given his consent to her being officially received at Court on, or soon after, her sixteenth birthday. The Emperor would officially inform the Court of Caroline's existence and explain why she had been brought up and educated away from the Court.

After this there were only a few more meetings between Caroline and her mother, and often they were very sad. The health of the Empress was getting more precarious, and she suffered much anxiety about the future of this young Archduchess.

The last time they met was at Nauheim, where three happy weeks were spent. In September, 1898, Frau von Friese, who was also in poor health, went to Denmark for one of her visits, and Caroline went away with her former guardians to remain with them for a few weeks before joining her mother in Switzerland.

And one fatal day in September, returning late to the hotel, without one word of warning, the hideous news was shouted into the ears of

the unprepared and unrecognised Princess—
" The Empress has been murdered."

Just that, nothing more or less.

For many days the shock of the ghastly
news rendered Caroline unconscious, and it is
believed for a very long time no one was able
to do anything with her.

She was taken back to Vienna by her guardian
and there news was received that Frau von
Friese was too ill to leave Denmark. In the
following December she died of cancer.

Then indeed Caroline, still unrecognised,
found herself bereft of all she loved. After
this second shock, she seemed to realise
the awfulness of her position, and began to
question her guardians as to plans for the
future.

They both told her that, until she had some
intimation from official quarters, it would be
most unwise for her, or indeed for themselves, to ask any questions. Meanwhile she
must content herself to live on as their
daughter, and they would do all they could to
make her happy.

And so some little time passed on in dreary
monotony, and terrible anguish for Caroline,

till one day she again questioned her guardian as to her future.

The poor girl seems to have been overwhelmed with reproaches for complaining, and was told in a very brutal and insinuating manner that it would be wiser for her to forget whose daughter she was, unless she wanted her mother's story to be in every one's mouth.

One can picture the blank astonishment, then the agonising despair with which the poor girl must have received this cruel accusation against her sainted mother.

There was apparently no one with whom she could speak freely. Her guardian's wife was not a woman in whom she could at that time confide any of her feelings, and nearly two years passed, during which time she seems to have bowed down to the law of silence imposed upon her, resolving firmly to bear all for the sake of her lost mother.

Very little attention was given to her, and apparently she was left as free as the ordinary young girl in society. But really she was kept under the strictest watch from the day of her mother's death. Everywhere she went she was followed by a detective, and generally by the

Police-Commissioner himself. This seems to point out that some one in high life wished to keep her always within sight.

In 1901 her guardian died, and Caroline felt his loss in more ways than one. He had always been a real friend, and had thoroughly followed out the instructions given by the Empress; whereas the attitude of his wife and daughter seemed to have changed entirely since the death of the Empress.

E

CHAPTER V

COUNTESS ZANARDI LANDI

IT was scarcely more than two weeks after her guardian's death, when Caroline began to feel, and perceive in every way, that her presence in the house was becoming very unwelcome. Hints were thrown out that it was quite time she married, and found a home of her own. Then commenced for her a still more unpleasant time, and in no direction could she turn for advice or consolation. There was no one to help and guide her. The peculiar circumstances in which she had been brought up prevented her from having made any real friendships.

The only young man of her acquaintance was Richard Kuhnelt, a lawyer, and a lieutenant, to whom she had always felt kindly disposed. One can imagine her astonishment, when matters were rapidly arranged between Frau

Photo, Langfier Ltd.

COUNTESS ZANARDI LANDI

Kuhnelt and her guardian, for a marriage between her and Richard Kuhnelt.

Indifference, and lack of courage to oppose anything, seem to have taken complete control of Caroline, and in a few days matters were finally arranged. In the wedding settlements it was found her mother had left her £160,000. This fact seems to have been concealed from her until then, and a well-known doctor, who had been appointed her guardian after the death of Herr ——, told her this money would be under the control of her future husband, as she was still under age.

In January, 1902, at the age of twenty, she married Richard Kuhnelt. Although there was no real love between these two, Caroline made a firm resolution to do everything she could to endure life as it was, and to do all in her power to make the home of her husband happy and peaceful.

Although surrounded by every luxury, and all that a young society woman could possibly desire, the marriage was not happy.

She had two children, Anthony Francis, born in 1902, and a little girl, Elizabeth Marie Christine, born in 1904.

Her husband seems to have been lured into bad speculations, and gradually their entire fortune was lost. In after years this ruin was found to have been brought about by those who knew of the existence of this unrecognised Princess.

Very soon there was only enough money left to buy a little house outside Vienna, where they lived for a while in absolute poverty.

But there came a worse time ; her husband had given up his work entirely, and fresh humiliations and disasters at length made her determine to leave Austria.

In 1906 they went to Canada, with only one servant, an old nurse for the two children.

For a year they tried living in Montreal, during which time Richard Kuhnelt seems to have treated his wife and children in a most heartless and brutal manner.

At last in 1908 they agreed to separate ; he went to New York, and Frau Kuhnelt took her two children and the nurse to try and begin a new life in British Columbia.

It is most interesting to hear from her own lips the trials and difficulties which she overcame in this wonderful land.

Photo. De Woolfe

ANTONIO FRANCIS AND MARIE CHRISTINE,
CHILDREN OF COUNTESS LANDI

At first this daughter of an Empress took the position of a cook at an hotel; then later on she took a little place, where she sold Viennese sweets and cakes, and for this she worked up quite a good connection.

So, with real hard toil, great determination and confidence that she must and would succeed for the sake of her children, she seems to have made for herself and them, in a very short time, sufficient to live on comfortably and happily.

And then, after some more months passed in Vancouver, she met her second husband, Count Zanardi Landi. From the first day of meeting, he proved a most kind and helpful counsellor; and it was he who advised her to try and assert her rights for the sake of her children, and above all for the sake of her dead mother.

It took nearly a year to obtain a divorce from Richard Kuhnelt; but finally everything was settled, and Frau Kuhnelt became the wife of Count Landi, who belongs to a well-known old Italian family.

In 1911 Count and Countess Landi, leaving the two children under the care of the old nurse, travelled to Europe with the fixed intention of trying to arrange for the real identification of the Countess.

They went direct to London; and before going to Vienna they visited Paris and Munich, so that they might wander around the parts so often visited by the late Empress.

It was a curious coincidence that there should be staying at the same hotel in Munich Queen Marie Sophia of Naples, one of the sisters of the Empress Elizabeth.

After some difficulty Countess Landi succeeded in gaining an interview with her aunt, who at first was not inclined to receive her, as she told her that, although she knew of her existence, it had been given out she had died some time ago.

With pictures of her little girl, and other identifications, she so convinced Queen Marie, that next day she requested Countess Landi to present her husband. After this they met several times, and the Queen promised to use her influence to put matters right at Court.

Endeavours were certainly made on the part of this aged aunt for her niece, but apparently no encouragement was met with from headquarters. In fact the Count and Countess left

Munich very soon, seeing that they would gain
no more material help from Queen Marie.

They next went to Vienna, and met many
old friends of the Countess, who all promised
to help her in every way. The assistance too
of a well-known Viennese lawyer was gained.
He it was who laid the entire matter before the
various heads of the department connected
with the Emperor's private cabinet.

Prince Montenuovo, and other officials at
Court seem to have gone thoroughly into the
matter ; many letters were written, and numerous interviews took place on behalf of the
Countess. Matters apparently received every
attention, and the lawyer left no stone un-
touched on her behalf.

Then the Countess received a vague reply, in
which it was stated that, as at that time the
Emperor's health was in rather a bad state, it
was thought advisable for the present to keep
the matter a secret. At the same time a
million and a half crowns was offered by the
Court to the Countess.

The Countess refused the money, once and
for all ; she wanted nothing but her birthright
accepted by her own family.

Next, it was proposed by Count Landi that they should go to his native land and seek advice there, and it was in Italy the idea was suggested that the story of her life should be written by the Countess herself, and put before the world.

Countess Landi is now living in London with her husband and her two children, perfectly happy and contented. She published some few months ago the story of her life, and before this great European War, she had met many members of the Viennese Court, including her sister, Archduchess Valérie, one and all of whom were doing their best to bring about her official recognition, as well as that of her children.

Countess Landi bears a striking resemblance to her mother, and she seems to possess all her delightful and fascinating qualities.

Since this dreadful War, she and her husband are untiring in their endeavours to help all those who have met misfortune through it, not by heading lists and subscribing to funds, but by finding out individual and deserving cases.

At Christmas time, I was reminded so much of the untiring and charitable Empress. There was the delightful Christmas-tree, arrayed as only the Austrians know how, laden with gifts, and prettily arranged.   Between twenty and thirty of the poorest families in London the Countess had invited to her house, given them a happy time, and to each some suitable gift.

In little Marie Christine, a charming child of eleven years, one sees a great likeness to her dead grandmother.   She is most clever and amusing, dances exquisitely and is already writing wonderful stories.   She has some lessons with a Russian lady, others with a French lady, and music is taught by a good professor.

Countess Landi, being so highly educated herself, has great ambitions for her children. She is particularly desirous that her little girl, whom she calls Mady, shall be a great linguist. Already she speaks French, German and English with perfect ease, and Russian is on the way.

" What was the real colour of the Empress's eyes and hair ? " I asked Countess Landi some little while ago.   " I have heard so many different accounts," I added.

" Ah," said Countess Landi, " my mother's eyes were just like Mady's, so difficult to describe, because the colour seems to change in various lights."

I turned to Mady, who has lovely eyes, and said:

" Mady has very deep blue eyes, surely ? "

" Yes," said Countess Landi, smiling in her delightful manner, " my mother's eyes were really a deep sapphire blue, which in some lights seemed almost amber ; and her hair was just the colour of chestnuts when they are lying on the ground."

Countess Landi's boy is already very tall and handsome, a typical Austrian, with a delightfully friendly nature. He goes at present to King Alfred's School ; probably later on he will go to one of our well-known Public Schools, where I am sure one will hear of his doing great things.

Countess Landi certainly inherits the gift of writing from her mother, and as one can gather from her wonderful book, *The Secret of an Empress*, she acquired the habit at an early age of writing down almost daily her impressions, and the various happenings of her eventful life. She is now very busy on her next work, which, I am sure, will be eagerly read by the English and American public.

CHAPTER VI

IMPERIAL CHILDREN

IT is some years ago since I met here, in London, Countess Hoyos, a well-known figure in Viennese society, and bearing the same name as that famous Count Hoyos who carried the fatal news to the Hofburg on the morning of the murder of the Crown Prince Rudolph.

Through her kindness, and great influence, I became attached to the suite of Archduke Karl Stefan, and passed some most delightful and interesting years at the Austrian Court.

I first spent some days with her in one of her beautiful old English country houses, where she most kindly instilled into me a few of the many hard-and-fast rules relating to the rigid etiquette of the Viennese Court. Then I left London to join the Imperial Family on their island in the Adriatic, a prey to various apprehensions, a distinct feeling of depression, and

59

a very limited knowledge of the German language.

It was the month of February when I arrived in Trieste, and took an Austrian Lloyd steamer down the Adriatic to Lussin, where I arrived about eleven o'clock at a tiny harbour with only two or three small lights flickering here and there.

I waited on deck, listening to the little crowd of jabbering Italians, until the captain had sent one of the officers to find some one who would have been sent to meet me.

Very soon I found myself being welcomed by His Excellency Count Chorinsky, the Lord Chamberlain to Archduke Karl Stefan, of whose charm, gallantry and kindness I had already heard so much from Countess Hoyos.

There are no roads, as such, on the island, consequently one is obliged to walk from the little harbour to Podjavori, the beautiful white villa of Their Imperial Highnesses.

I remember I found it extremely amusing and somewhat embarrassing this last part of my journey, the walk of thirty minutes at least, along a rugged, stony mountainous pathway, by the sea which beat up on the great rocks, meeting not a soul, and with no light but the occasional switch of the electric torch of my guide.

Very close behind us rattled a little luggage cart, drawn by a pair of donkeys, the only animals on the island, who were continually being shouted at, and hurried on by two gesticulating Italian servants.

At last, breathless and somewhat tired, having climbed nearly half-way up Monte Jovanni, we arrived at our destination, where I was received by Countess Huyn, lady-in-waiting to Archduchess Maria Theresa; the house director, Herr Schussel; and an Italian maid, Didarc, who always waited on me when the Imperial household was in residence at Lussin.

Countess Huyn was gaiety and charm personified, and seemed to know exactly how I was feeling—tired, excited, and dubious after four days' travelling to an unknown and strange land. But she laughed it all away, as she led me to my room, where, with many kindly handshakes, she bade me good night.

The next morning I was awakened by Didarc, who was throwing back the green shutters to let in the glorious sunshine of one of those perfect mornings which are only to be found in the South.

Notwithstanding the warmth and sunshine already pouring into the room, the maid hastened to pile logs of wood into the quaint stove, made of stone, which is a peculiar feature in every Austrian household.

After a delicious breakfast had been brought to me of coffee, rolls and cakes—is there any country where one finds such an appetising repast as an Austrian breakfast ?—I was beginning to wonder when the summons would come to make my curtsy to the Imperial Family, when a knock came to my door. A little lady dressed in mourning came in, and introduced herself as the Ober-Gouvernante of the young Archduchesses Eleonore and Renata.

In a very friendly voice she bade me welcome, and asked me to accompany her to the presence of Her Imperial Highness Archduchess Maria Theresa.

I was already in calling costume, as I could see from my windows that my rooms were in an *annexe* in the grounds, a little distant from the main building, so catching up some white kid gloves—which had been impressed upon me so often as being the chief necessity of life at Court—I prepared to follow Fräulein von Baender.

We encountered various personages of the suite, and many servants, nearly all Italians, who always stood still and bowed low until we passed.

On entering the villa, a very long, low stone erection, built on terraces on the side of the mountain, we passed up a very wide flight of grey marble steps, leading out of a cool delightful stone vestibule, to the corridor along which ran the suite of apartments of the Archduke and Archduchess.

At one of a number of doors, all exactly alike, Fräulein von Baender turned to me and said :

" This is the ante-chamber of Her Imperial Highness, which we shall walk through to the boudoir. I will leave you at the entrance. Her Imperial Highness awaits you ; please remember to curtsy and kiss her hand."

Almost immediately I was in a pretty flower-filled apartment, bowing low before a very

tall and imposing woman, who was standing
painting before a large easel.

She received me with an embarrassed and
nervous smile ; and, as I bent and kissed her
hand, she made a few pleasant remarks in
slow and halting English.

I remember she seemed to be so much more
nervous and shy than I was, that I found
myself helping her out with her sentences,
until I suddenly recalled myself to the fact that
one must never lead or interrupt the conversation of an Imperial Highness.

Presently she asked me to accompany her, to
be presented to the young Archdukes and Archduchesses, and we went through many charming,
but very simply furnished apartments, all
leading out of each other, to the sitting-room
used by Archduchesses Eleonore and Renata.

We found them both feeding some birds, but
immediately on our entrance they came quickly
forward to kiss their mother's hand. Then they
both shook me warmly by the hand, in a very
friendly fashion, asking me about my journey,
in fluent English.

Archduchess Eleonore, a tall, fair girl with
attractive manners, had her hair closely braided

round her head, and was dressed very simply in black. In fact, every one was in mourning for some reigning prince, or duke, and I quickly found how very often anyone attached to an Imperial entourage is plunged into black.

Archduchess Renata, famous for her likeness to her beautiful cousin, the murdered Empress, was also most frank and natural, and wore her gloriously curly hair in two heavy plaits reaching to her knees. She had wonderful eyes, which lit up with fiery darts as she spoke in an impulsive and reckless manner, and, of all the family, she was the one whose temperament most resembled that of the late Empress, and who gave to all those with whom she came in contact many difficult and perplexing moments.

On leaving these two young Archduchesses— who both curtsied and again kissed the hand of their mother—we went to another apartment furnished exactly as the others. Here we found the little Archduchess Mechtildis, who was rather delicate-looking but very pretty, with much fluffy fair hair; she was attended by Mademoiselle Seifert, her governess.

I next accompanied Her Imperial Highness up another low flight of stone steps, where

F

were the rooms of the remaining three children. Archduke Karl was an exceedingly good-looking boy of about fourteen years of age, whose English was also fluent, and cultured ; he was attended by Captain Lyst, who accompanied him everywhere and overlooked the arrangements of his studies.

Then the two small Archdukes Willi and Leo we found in a delightful big airy room at the end of the corridor, preparing to walk out with Fräulein Wienke. Their tutor, Herr Saller, had just left them ; he worked with them from eight o'clock each morning, both the boys having had breakfast at 7.30 a.m.

Besides the tutors and governesses already mentioned, I subsequently learnt there were the following : Herr Theodorovitch, the Polish tutor, Captain Cohanyi, a naval officer, who instructed the young Archdukes in mathematics and Hungarian, and the chaplain, who gave religious instruction to all the Imperial children, and taught several German subjects to Archduke Karl. Music was taught by Frau Drost, who had very little difficulty in making a brilliant musician of the Archduchess Renata.

This somewhat large retinue of four resident

ladies and four resident gentlemen, solely for
the education of these Imperial children, was
chosen by the Archduke himself from the upper
middle-classes, so that they might have plenty
of healthy outside influence, and it struck me
as being very carefully thought out for a member
of the much-abused Hapsburg family.

Quite recently I met a lady well-known at the
Court of Vienna, who was staying with Archduchess Renata, married to Prince Radziwill
just before the war broke out. She most
indignantly protested against the idea that
this family was tainted with madness or degeneracy, and went on to say that it was with
the idea of fighting against any too much blue
blood that wet nurses were installed for the
children as babies.

Both Their Imperial Highnesses were averse
to the notion of marriages being arranged for
the three Archduchesses; in fact, I have heard
the Archduke say that, although they were all
very wealthy Archduchesses, no marriages
should be forced upon them, and hence we learn
of at least three exceptionally ideal marriages
having taken place in a Hapsburg family.

After this most interesting tour of inspection,

I was invited to accompany one of the Archduchesses and her governess for a walk in the
grounds.

I made my obeisance to Archduchess Maria
Theresa and again kissed her hand; and we
prepared to descend into the garden by way of
one of the broad terraces.

CHAPTER VII

ADMIRAL ARCHDUKE KARL STEFAN

I DO not think I shall easily forget that morning in February, as we stood for a while on the terrace of the Palazzo Podjavori—one of Archduke Karl Stefan's southern villas on the island Lussin—whilst Archduchess Eleonore pointed out to me one or two points of interest.

It was intensely warm. A brilliant sun blazed down from a cloudless blue sky, and far away the rocky and wonderful garden stretched down the mountain-side to the edge of the blue Adriatic.

The air was laden with the scents of orange and citron-trees, roses and mimosa, and a faint hum of insect life murmured about one's ears, as the lizards darted hither and thither; life on that little rocky island seemed a dream of delight.

There was no straight bit in the garden,

except the tennis-court, with tall palm-trees at one end, and raised seats, built under shady mimosa-trees. Here we at last encountered Admiral Archduke Karl Stefan busily talking to two or three of his Italian gardeners.

He seemed to see us approaching from some little distance, for he abruptly turned from the men and called up to us as we were descending a winding rocky path :

" Good morning. I'm delighted to meet you. Hope you have had a good journey."

By this time he was shaking me most heartily by the hand, in a very friendly and delightful manner.

Archduchess Eleonore, who I afterwards learnt was his favourite, ran forward and kissed his hand, saying :

" Isn't it jolly, papa, the Miss Nellie plays tennis. Can't we all play this afternoon ? "

" Oh, capital ! " said the Archduke impulsively. " Let's play at once." And turning to the men he shouted in Italian, " Antonio, Carlo, quick—balls—fetch the markers."

There were always ready for tennis four Dalmatian boys, in their picturesque national dress, who were made to stand at each corner

of the court, holding in their hands strong
nets attached to long poles, with which they
picked up the balls. There were at least two
or three dozen balls, and the boys were adepts
with their nets in catching, and gathering up
the balls, which they as quickly flung into
large baskets arranged at a convenient height
for the players, at each end of the tennis
place.

"Oh, but, papa," pleaded Archduchess
Eleonore, smiling up at her impetuous father,
"how can we play *now?* The Miss has scarcely
unpacked, I'm sure, and there is no one ready."

"We shall play now," said His Imperial
Highness, his tall figure already half-way up one
of the paths. "Tell the Count and Lieutenant
——, or one of the men, to find a fourth. I
shall be back in two minutes."

Such was the Archduke. We were all hurrying back to the house ; already I saw several
servants rushing along, and by the time we
reached the vestibule commotion reigned, all
because His Imperial Highness commanded
tennis to be played at 11.30 in the morning.

"But *déjeuner* is at twelve o'clock," said a
worried footman, as I hurried to my annexe.

I too was worried and perplexed, and oh, so repentant that I had mentioned tennis ! How soon I learnt to be more careful of what I said when the Archduke was nigh.

Then I ran up three steps at a time when I reached the villa, fearing to be late, and nearly knocked over Count Chorinsky, and a tall, very good-looking military officer.

"Oh, you English !" said the gay Count, shaking his head at me, and trying not to look very much disturbed and annoyed. "I can see the Mees is beginning to bring trouble on her head." I tried to explain and apologise, but it was impossible. "No ! No ! even an Imperial luncheon hour must be changed because the English Mees demands tennis in the morning," he went on mockingly. "May I present Captain Lyst to you ? "

Immediately with a profound bow, and the clicking of spurred heels, the mocking eyes of Archduke Karl's aide-de-camp were lowered, and he kissed my hand, saying in broken English, "I speak—only—three words—dat is—I lof you."

Still more worried and perplexed, I reached my room, and threw myself into a tennis rig-up.

Seizing my racket, I very soon found myself playing a very hard set with Count Chorinsky against the Archduke and Lieutenant ——.

It was a splendid game. The Archduke played a masterly stroke, but I soon discovered he was a bad loser.

We played three sets without interruption, and I entirely gave myself up to the joys of the game. I remember a loud-sounding gong rang three times up at the house, and the major-domo came to the entrance of the court, dressed in a gorgeous livery of crimson and silver, and wearing white gloves. He bowed very low, and asked the Archduke, in German, whether His Imperial and Royal Highness would be pleased to hear that luncheon was served, and that Their Imperial Highnesses awaited his pleasure.

No notice was taken of this, and gradually it dawned on me that Count Chorinsky and Lieutenant —— were becoming manifestly uneasy, so, when a fourth set was proposed, being accustomed to speak freely, I said very frankly :

" Shall we not postpone our game until after lunch, as the gong has sounded twice ? "

Blank looks of surprise and relief were seen

on the faces of the two men, and the Archduke said carelessly :

" It can't possibly be twelve o'clock yet. What *is* the time, Chorinsky ? " he said, throwing his racquet to one of the attendants, and mopping his face.

" Please, Your Imperial Highness, it is a quarter to one."

" Great heavens ! " said the Archduke. " This is all through the Miss—she would insist on playing," he said laughingly to me. " Well, come along to lunch."

It was indeed a dreadful moment for me. My heart literally froze, as I encountered a cold and silent group standing about in the vestibule. No one spoke as we came up, and through a mist I saw a curtsying crowd.

" Begin, begin," said the Archduke impatiently. " I shall be down directly."

Then two great doors were flung open, and a row of servants stood bowing silently, as the procession moved solemnly into a long, low dining-hall, leading off from the right of the lounge.

To-day I look back on that meeting with His Imperial Highness, in the sunny and peaceful island Lussin in the blue Adriatic. Some few weeks ago only, that little dream island was awakened by mine explosions, the booming of guns, and all the hideous accompaniment of naval warfare.

At the beginning of this great European War the command of the Austrian Navy was given into the very capable hands of Admiral Archduke Karl Stefan, cousin of the Emperor of Austria, nephew of Marie Henriette, Queen of the Belgians, and brother of Queen Christina of Spain.

He is a man of extraordinary genius, with an infinite knowledge of all matters nautical, and possessing the wonderful gift of being able to converse equally well in English, French, German, Italian, Polish and Hungarian. He is considerably over six feet, an adept at skating, dancing and tennis, and has two hobbies, of which he is passionately fond—painting and music.

I have heard his rendering of Chopin compared to that of Paderewski, and many a time I have sat amongst an audience spellbound by the passion and intensity of his marvellous playing.

It is of interest to note that besides his

beautiful palace in Vienna he owns big estates, forest lands and shooting-boxes in Galicia, and an old historic Polish castle called Zywiec not far from Cracow, now the scene of fighting between the Russians, Germans and Austrians.

He also owns a palace in Pola, and some years ago built a winter palace in Lussin, both of which are now amidst scenes of naval battles, mine explosions and the continual roar of the cannon.

Besides these sumptuous palaces, Archduke Karl Stefan is never without a steam yacht, always in readiness in the harbour at Lussin, to take His Imperial Highness and suite, either to some remote Eastern waters or, perchance, to cruise about in home waters, the ever-beautiful Adriatic.

Archduke Karl Stefan is one of the wealthy Hapsburgs, closely related to the Emperor, and to the late Archduke Albrecht, son of the famous Archduke Karl, the great general who defeated Napoleon at Aspern.

His mother, Archduchess Elizabeth, to whom he was devotedly attached, died in February, 1903. Of all her children she was specially proud of Karl Stefan and Queen Christina of

Spain, who bear a strong resemblance to each other in features and character, both being fair, with blue eyes, and the remarkable Hapsburg nose and jaw. In early days, each tried to outdo the other in wild games, practical jokes, and tricks so boisterous that those in charge had the greatest difficulty in keeping them within reasonable bounds.

Archduke Friedrich, the eldest brother of Karl Stefan, is the richest of the Hapsburgs, and a great speculator; he is now one of those in command of the Austrian army.

His wife is Archduchess Isabella, and it was to their daughter that the late Heir-Apparent was supposed to be paying attention, when he fell in love with the lady-in-waiting, Countess Chotek.

Archduke Friedrich owns the magnificent and gorgeous Palais Friedrich in Vienna, the palatial building joining and communicating with the Hofburg.

Before he built and designed his present Palace in the Wiednerhaupt Strasse, Archduke Karl Stefan and suite used to reside in one half of this building when visiting Vienna.

Another brother of Karl Stefan's, one of the

tallest and handsomest men in Vienna, is Archduke Eugene, a great soldier, and a man possessing strong religious views.

Archduchess Marie Henriette, wife of the late King of the Belgians, is a sister to Archduchess Elizabeth, his mother. Stéphanie, his cousin, is the least attractive member of this family; and, though the young Archduchesses often spoke of their " Tante Stéphanie," they never showed much love or interest in this particular relative.

CHAPTER VIII

SOME CHARACTERISTICS OF ARCHDUKE
KARL STEFAN

SO much has been written about the Hapsburg family, their madness, degeneracy, and eccentricities, that I think, by a close study of this particular branch of the family, namely, that of Archduke Karl Stefan, and his relatives—many of whom I know personally, and for whom I cherish a great admiration and respect—my readers will be forced to conclude that many of the tales one reads are a great exaggeration. It is necessary to have met, to have spoken with some of these most interesting Austrian Archdukes and Archduchesses, before one can in the least realise, or understand their peculiarities, the extraordinary position they hold, and their difficult surroundings.

It is not wise or fair to condemn the entire Hapsburg family because of the various rather too well-known escapades one continually reads about. The bare facts, very often entirely misconstrued, are seen in print, and the real circumstances of the case, known only to a very few, seldom appear.

Archduke Karl Stefan married Archduchess Maria Theresa, granddaughter of the old King of Naples, and first cousin to the murdered Crown Prince Franz Ferdinand; her mother, Archduchess Immaculata, and his mother were sisters.

She is a wonderful woman, full of charm and self-control, devoting much of her energy and time, now that her children are grown up, to the care of the poor. Just recently she could be seen going from hospital to hospital in Vienna, nursing the sick and wounded, under the name of Sister Michaelis. Her sister, Princess Caroline, is married to Prince August of Saxe-Coburg, and her other sister married Duke Robert of Würtemberg.

Maria Theresa is a splendid wife for the Archduke, who possesses such a restless and versatile temperament. She is so calm, quiet and self-possessed, and always ready to fall in with the many whims and unexpected movements of her erratic husband.

ARCHDUCHESS MARIA THERESA

He has a great admiration for England, and all things English, and during the years I spent at the Austrian Court I received much attention and kindness from the Archduke.

He would discuss all kinds of subjects with me ; and I was often called upon to give my opinion on matters of decoration and arrangement of the Imperial yachts, or the rooms of the Castle or Palace.

He had a wonderful artistic imagination ; and, although many of his yachts were designed and built in England, much of the planning and most of the ideas were his own.

He had a great craze for rearranging and changing his surroundings. Unfortunately for me, he found out one day that I possessed a certain amount of originality, and that I was scarcely ever known to leave the furnishing and general arrangements of the many delightful suites of rooms I occupied, in the different palaces, as first I found them.

Nothing that is said or done at the Austrian Court remains long unnoticed, one very soon learns.

I remember one particular afternoon at Zywiec Castle ; it was a gala day, one of the

G

Archduchess's birthdays, I believe, and the entire Imperial Family was spending a quiet hour *en famille* in the private apartments of the Archduke. I was preparing to go for a long ramble in the park, when suddenly a peremptory knock at my door was heard, and to my "*Herein!*" there entered one of the Court lackeys in his gorgeous livery, one who is generally sent on messages of great importance. "His Imperial and Royal Highness wishes your presence at once in His Highness's private study."

Amazement and astonishment must have been plainly written on my countenance. It was not customary for any of the suite to join the family on these occasions.

The servant silently withdrew, with the usual low bow, and I hastily disrobed and searched round for a quick change into suitable garb. Then in nervous haste, and fearing I know not what, I went the endless length of corridors and rooms to the Archduke's apartment.

I went through the ante-chamber, guided by the voices beyond, and entered the huge, delightfully cosy room where all the Imperial Family was assembled.

" What can they want ? " I thought to myself,

as I stood for a second inside the entrance, making my lowest bow.

" Oh, there you are, at last ! " said the Archduke, coming across to me in an excited and eager way. " Now, look *well* round, and tell me what you think ? I have entirely rearranged the whole place—moved everything. As you have such wonderful ideas on alterations, and readjustments," he said with a very amused look at me, " tell me if it is an improvement."

I looked round bewildered ; certainly Her Imperial Highness and the young Archduchesses and Archdukes, and the one or two servants standing round, all looked very hot, and flushed with recent exertions.

I had only arrived at the Castle a few days before, and as I had not seen this particular suite of rooms, it was a difficult problem. But knowing the Archduke already, and seeing the expectant look on the faces of all around, I felt instantly I must live up to my apparent reputation.

I took another hurried glance round, and then assured the Archduke that, in my humble opinion, the room could not be arranged to better advantage. Then, fortunately, at that moment I caught sight of an enormous screen, of most beautiful Eastern design and workmanship.

"Would not Your Imperial Highness try the effect of that lovely old screen in this alcove, with the light falling on it?"

Instantly there was a chorus of delight from all; something else to move—oh, the fascination of it all! It did one good to see them. And it took quite another half-hour to move it round, change it again, and find yet another improvement!

Alas, the next afternoon, as we were all coming up the big stone staircase, leading from the blue vestibule, where tea had been taken at the various small tables dotted over this charming hall, the Archduke called up to me:

"Oh, if you are doing nothing particular, I am coming to see the latest improvements in your rooms!"

Thinking this was only said in a mocking, teasing way, with no intention of carrying the idea out, I replied that I should be honoured and delighted to receive a visit from His Imperial Highness.

As I was sitting writing in the extreme corner of my sitting-room, not five minutes later, in walked the Archduke, after a short sharp knock at my door.

"Oh, I have brought you a dozen or so of English novels," said the Archduke, as he dropped quite fourteen or fifteen Tauchnitz editions of English works on to my huge Chesterfield. "Now," he added, looking round, and smiling very mischievously, "I don't like the way you have this place arranged at all, it's most inartistic; do let me make a few suggestions."

And, before I had recovered from my amusement and astonishment, he had picked up one or two Persian rugs from the beautiful polished oak floor, and opening the door flung them out in the corridor.

He then proceeded to push the bigger pieces of furniture from the corners of the room all into the centre, and before I could protest, or make myself understood, the entire contents of the enormous room were standing huddled up in the centre of the room, looking exactly like a store-room in a furniture shop.

"Now," said the Archduke, "having put everything in the centre, we can proceed to plan out."

" But," I said, when I had recovered from my laughter, and had made myself heard and seen—because the large pieces of furniture were put one above the other, and prevented my seeing the Archduke, who was wedged in between the wall and furniture—" Your Imperial Highness is most kind and amiable to take so much trouble. I am perfectly content with this room as it is, and should anyone, Her Imperial Highness for instance, happen to come this way, she would be so very much astonished —and——"

Just at that moment a knock was heard at one of my doors, and turning my head I saw Archduchess Maria Theresa peering through one of the doors.

" Oh, Miss Nellie, I beg your pardon, but is anything the matter ? Your carpets are all outside the door, and——"

The Archduchess paused, as she came farther into the room, with a look of blank amazement, as at first she did not see the Archduke, who kept himself well hidden on the other side.

" Oh, Your Imperial Highness must please excuse this muddle," I began in a confused voice.

" Yes," interrupted the Archduke, laughing

and thoroughly enjoying the absurd situation, "we are overhauling the room, and making a completely new arrangement."

The Archduchess rose to the occasion at once, as she always did, and burst out laughing.

"Really it is too bad to worry the Miss like this ; you are upsetting her room entirely, and it will take quite a long time to put straight."

Just then there passed along the corridor Count Chorinsky, who was evidently searching the Castle for the Archduke. He paused before the open door, and of course came hurriedly forward seeing the Archduke, whom he was seeking. With a look of surprise at the funny group, he said, bowing low to the Archduke, that a special messenger had arrived and wished to speak to His Imperial Highness, with reference to the hunt on the morrow.

The Archduke, entirely forgetting my room, and the confusion caused, and ever eager for fresh topics—if they happen to please—walked rapidly away with the Count, talking and gesticulating violently.

My room and its contents were forgotten ; but I was thankful for the interruption.

And during all my stay at the Imperial Court,

a new improvement, an alteration, a new design was always brought to my notice by this extraordinarily active and abnormally clever Archduke.

I must not forget to refer to that other side of Karl Stefan's character, the quiet, studious side, when for hours at a time he would be found, in an out-of-the-way corner, painting some exquisite view—generally a wild desolate scene, where some wonderful bit of colour had struck his artistic eye.

He would rise at five or six o'clock in the morning, wearing his painter's uniform, which was generally a pair of old brown, very baggy corduroy trousers, a holland jacket, and an enormous hat—very often a tea-planter's hat. He would then set forth with a large canvas under his arm, and one of his servants carrying the painting apparatus.

For hours and hours he would work away, and meals were never thought about. He was always quite pleased for anyone to stand and watch him paint, it never seemed to bother him, but he did not care to talk much. He had rather a funny habit, whilst working or thinking deeply, of singing or humming in a low kind of voice, never any particular melody, just a quaint sing-song tune confined to one or two notes only. It was a very remarkable sound, and one which carried quite a distance, so that it was always possible to know, within a little, in which direction the Archduke would be found working at his canvas.

Sometimes he would go off on his yacht, merely on a painting cruise, very often taking with him some well-known artist ; then he would return suddenly after a few weeks' absence, bringing back some exquisite results.

The Archduke was very good too in sending, or lending his works to exhibitions, or small *salons*.

Two of his sons, Archduke Karl and Archduke Leo, have inherited the same great talent in painting, sketching and designing ; but only one of his children, Archduchess Renata, possesses that other remarkable accomplishment, of being able to perform so extraordinarily well on the piano. She certainly has the same great love of music, and like her father would sit for hours at a time playing the most intricate of classical music, putting her whole heart and soul into the instrument, from which she brought forth sounds full of pathos and passionate feeling.

CHAPTER IX

EDUCATION AND MARRIAGE OF THE
IMPERIAL CHILDREN

THE system of education of an Imperial Archduke and Archduchess is most strenuous and thorough; and they are made to work really very hard all the year round.

There are no long holidays at Christmas and Easter, merely the actual feast days, and perhaps the two following days.

In the summer the children are free from actual studies, generally speaking, during the months of July and August; but even through these months the different languages—in which they are extraordinarily proficient—must be practised and studied to a certain extent.

Usually studies begin at an early age with Imperial children; and at the age of five or six years they can read and write remarkably well.

90

English, French, German and Italian were spoken and understood by all the children of Archduke Karl Stefan from a very early age. All these languages were used in general conversation throughout the entire day ; and the rapidity with which they skipped, as it were, from one language to another was amazing.

I was at first astounded at the regularity of their day's work.

Generally at half-past seven—and very often at seven in the summer—a light breakfast was taken, consisting merely of coffee, rolls and cakes.

Before this, Mass was attended in the private chapel, so that it was obvious the children rose about six o'clock each morning. By half-past seven or eight o'clock, each Archduke and Archduchess was well at work with his or her respective professor. I have remarked before, that in this particular family, there were eight members of the educational staff, besides the various visiting teachers.

At ten o'clock the Imperial children partook of sandwiches and a glass of wine, after which a walk in the private grounds was taken with a foreign professor, during which time French,

English or Polish was spoken, or whatever the nationality of the professor happened to be.

The Imperial child during this hour was on his or her word of honour to speak only in that language, and the rule was most strictly enforced and adhered to.

From eleven to twelve o'clock, another hour of study took place, and about five minutes before the hour there would be a hurried rush to the various dressing-rooms, where their different maids or valets would be waiting anxiously to make their Imperial charges respectable for the luncheon.

This was a long and formal meal, which took place in the great dining-hall of the Château.

It was very lengthy, and consisted of a most elaborate menu ; while every kind of delicacy and luxury was seen on this festive board.

As cooking in Austria is an absolute art, even in bourgeois families—and not in the least degree after the style of the Germans, who are quite content with quantity alone—one can imagine that in that of an Imperial house of Austria, and especially in that of Karl Stefan, who has traversed the whole world, the excellence and splendour of the table are not to be rivalled.

One is at first surprised that wine is so freely drunk at meals, even by young children. It is quite the custom to see, at these long and elaborate luncheons and dinners, a young Archduke and Archduchess of seven or eight years, each of course attended by his or her professor. In the case of an Archduchess of sixteen or seventeen years of age, there is also present her lady-in-waiting.

The luncheon generally occupies an hour or more; and I have sat over two hours at an Imperial luncheon, when there have been many guests and the menu has been especially elaborate.

Usually these meals are solemn and very stately, and conversation very studied. Either His or Her Imperial Highness leads the conversation, and one does not make casual remarks, or try to keep up conversation, unless especially addressed.

Immediately after this function, drives in the neighbouring forest, tennis or skating takes place until 3.30, when *goûter* is served on some terrace, or in a small hall, and is more or less the informal meal of the day. At no table in the world are served more delicious, richer or daintier cakes and sweets than at an Austrian table.

From a quarter to four until the dressing bell rings at a quarter to seven, lessons are again in full swing. Then every one dons a more or less elaborate evening toilette, and another long and stately repast takes one till eight o'clock. When dinner is over, one lingers for about twenty minutes, standing about in the rooms adjoining the dining-hall, after which every one curtsies low before Their Imperial Highnesses, the children kiss their hands, and at this early hour every one retires.

The procession to and from a meal strikes one as being excessively tedious. One must always be so extremely careful that the order of precedence is strictly carried out, and that one walks on the left-hand side of a superior.

First there is the assembling, and generally a long period of waiting for the young Archdukes and Archduchesses, their attendants and the lords and ladies-in-waiting, and finally appears Archduchess Maria Theresa, after which there is generally another very long wait for Archduke Karl Stefan.

The three young Princesses, although made to work at their studies very hard, all enjoyed a delightful and varied life. From an early age they were taught to love the sea, and delightful cruises to foreign lands were taken each year, on their father's magnificent steam yacht.

Four glorious months, from January to April, were spent on their beautiful island in the sunny South, then followed generally a two months' voyage to some distant land.

Late summer and autumn was spent in their magnificent Polish château, amongst the forest lands, within sight of the great heights of the Tatra; and, sandwiched in between these delightful wanderings, short visits were paid to the gay capital where operas, theatres, concerts and balls were all equally enjoyed by these three gay and delightful Princesses.

Renata was the first to marry. She was often spoken of as one of the Emperor's favourite young cousins, because of her great resemblance to the late Empress, and because of her high spirits and unruly nature.

Her choice met with the approval of the Emperor and her parents ; and, although not a prince of the Austrian Imperial House, Prince Jerome Radziwill belongs to the highest Polish nobility. He was educated by the Jesuits in Switzerland, is a most exemplary young man, and most popular in Cracow. I heard not long ago that, should there be a King of Poland, the people themselves would gladly welcome Prince Jerome as their ruler.

There are three branches of this great Radziwill family, the Russian, the German and the Austrian-Polish. He, of course, belongs to the last-mentioned.

Archduchess Renata married in 1909, and lives a great part of the year at the Château Balice at Zaburzow in Galicia, about twenty miles from the borderland of Russia.

It was very interesting to hear from a friend of mine, who was staying with the Princess Renata Radziwill three years ago, that even then the borderland was mined, and barbed wire was arranged half a mile deep along the frontier. In the low-lying land along the Vistula, barbed wire traps were laid, and mounds of grass along the hills concealed large guns.

All this was seen by my friend, and pointed out to her as precautions already then taken against a Russian invasion.

Princess Renata Radziwill had also been asked by the authorities if she would give the Castle for use as a hospital. All the rooms were counted, and the matter thoroughly gone into even in 1912.

The horses owned by every one were counted periodically by the Government; and on certain days the peasants and owners of horses were obliged to bring their animals into the towns to be examined and counted, as all are requisitioned in time of war.

The marriage of Princess Renata Radziwill is an absolutely happy one; and she has three perfectly charming children.

Archduchess Mechtildis, the youngest girl, married in 1914 another Polish Prince, which marriage was one of her own choice, and has also met with Imperial approval.

Prince Olgierd Czartoryski is a distinguished Prince of the old Polish nobility, and they are devotedly attached to each other. The marriage was celebrated at the private chapel of the Imperial château in Zywiec, and was attended

H

by a large gathering of Archdukes and Arch-duchesses, and many high Polish families. Archduke Friedrich represented the Emperor, and Queen Christina of Spain, the aunt of the bride, was also present.

Much surprise and a great deal of comment was caused by the marriages of these two younger sisters before the eldest girl.

But Archduchess Eleonore had been secretly engaged to the handsome and dashing commander of her father's yacht, Lieutenant von Kloss, for at least five years.

Many offers from princes of the Royal house and of other lands had all been refused by this extremely tall, slight and attractive Archduchess.

For the last few years she had shown a strong disinclination for Court life, but was never tired of long sea voyages on her father's beautiful yacht.

The secret of her love was discovered only when Archduchess Eleonore wrote one day to a cousin, telling of her romantic attachment; in the same letter she seems to have written very strongly of her determination to marry no one but the man of her choice.

As soon as they learned their daughter's secret, the parents of the Archduchess, who were unable to give their sanction or consent, put the matter before the Emperor without delay.

Lieutenant von Kloss was thirty-two years of age, and most popular with his fellow-officers ; he has had a very rapid and successful career, and belongs to an old and distinguished Silesian family.

The Emperor, when he found the inquiries which he caused to be made entirely satisfactory, summoned the Lieutenant to an audience and gave a willing consent.

The marriage took place last year at Zywiec, and was a strictly family celebration.

The Archduchess had to relinquish her rank and rights as a member of the House of Hapsburg, and is now known as Frau von Kloss.

She had numerous and costly presents from many royal and distinguished people. On her wedding-day she looked a vision of loveliness, and seemed bubbling over with love and happiness.

Her married life so far has been perfectly happy.

They bought, and furnished very simply, a charming villa in Pola, and everything that tends to luxury is sternly repressed.

She is the same gay and jolly Archduchess; you could see her walking out in simple tailor-made gowns, with no affectation, just enjoying life. As she says, with her merry laugh, " I am only the wife of a simple officer."

But at night this simple ex-Archduchess dresses herself in radiant fabrics, beautiful brocades and fairy-like chiffons, rare old lace and priceless jewels, for in her trousseau her generous and loving parents showered gifts, just as for a marriage with a prince.

Just before her marriage she wrote to me the following lines in English, which seem to express so well her truly happy and joyous frame of mind :

Dear Mrs Ryan, I am so pleased with the kind words you sent me and I thank you most earnestly for your letter and congratulations. My fiancé – naval officer – is a splendid man, so kindhearted and generous. He has all the qualities to make me most happy. I am awfully happy already!!

My marriage will be together with Titsch on the 11. January at Zywiec in our chapel.

My fiancé is embarked just now so I cant see him very often. We shall live at Pola. I am sure you know the place from the time you spent with us.

I shall send you later on my photo together with my fiancé: Will that do? To which address?

Many kind regards and heartfelt thanks from yours truly Eleanor

So it is indeed possible, and very true, that even Hapsburgs can be happy, wise and good ; marriages, too, with them, can be of their own choosing, and still be successful love matches.

CHAPTER X

ACHILLEION, THE FORMER RESIDENCE OF
ELIZABETH, NOW OWNED BY THE GERMAN
EMPEROR

JUST as Heligoland is to-day a prize of
strategic worth to the German Emperor,
so indeed may be Achilleion, recently
acquired by him, and once the favourite
residence of the Empress of Austria. Whether
it only remains famous in history as one of the
most luxurious and artistic royal residences
ever designed and created, or whether it is to
serve some sinister purpose in the present
European War, remains to be seen.

On one occasion, in the early summer, when
the Imperial yacht was stationed at Corfu,
I was one of the suite to accompany Archduke
Karl Stefan, and Archduchess Maria Theresa,
to visit this wonderful Grecian palace at Corfu.

The drive from the harbour of nearly two
hours, through the most magnificent moun-

tainous scenery, brought us to the gates of the great park.

Here we all alighted, as there was no means of driving to the house, it being one of the particular whims of the Empress that all approaches to the house by strangers should be made on foot.

Only those who have actually visited the Achilleion will know that to drive up any of the mountainous rocky paths is almost an impossibility, as the ascent to the house, built on the natural formation of the rock, is a most difficult feat to accomplish.

"*Gott im Himmel!*" exclaimed the Archduke, as we all toiled along, breathless and exhausted, "it's twenty minutes since we left the gates, and we seem only half-way up. I have often *heard* of the extraordinary energy and love of exercise my poor cousin possessed, but never until to-day have I believed its truth. Let us all rest here by this little Greek temple, whilst the men of the party gather some of the precious fruit, for which this Eden is said to be famous."

And for a time we rested on the steps of the red marble staircase leading to the temple,

THE EXTERIOR OF ACHILLEION, CORFU

containing the superb statue of Heine, which the Empress Elizabeth had erected to her favourite poet. This had been so cleverly placed that it seemed to spring out from the luxuriant greenery, and look down far below into the blue expanse of the calm Grecian waters.

"Here—just here," said the Archduke, pausing on the top step and removing his hat before entering this shelter of memories, "Her Majesty used to sit for whole days, a mournful crape-clad woman, plunged in the depths of grief; she came last in 1896, filled with a ghastly presentiment she would never see it again. Poor Elizabeth, so cruelly wronged and misjudged! *Mad* they called her because of all *this*, because a woman, with a great artistic soul, and a passionate love of the sea, succeeds in thinking out, designing and creating this dream palace, and chooses consolation from all social noise and turmoil in such a—paradise," and the Archduke paused, because he was unable to find words fit enough to describe the most beautiful spot on God's earth. "Let us get on to the house itself," he added, "that, I am told, cost millions of pounds, and was built by an Italian architect entirely after her own designs. What a brain—colossal!"

And then, suddenly, it burst upon us—that magnificent white marble edifice, with its loggias and balconies crowning the rocky heights, a proof of what her artistic sense really was.

We found ourselves at the principal entrance, which is supported by twelve marble columns, and adorned with some precious statues brought from Rome by the Empress herself. On the inner walls of this magnificent peristyle, the Archduke pointed out paintings by Greek masters, and frescoes by great Italian painters. This is connected with a sumptuously decorated *salon*, a beautiful little chapel, a dining-hall and the main entrance-hall, containing priceless treasures of art, rugs, tapestries and lamps, all brought from the East. Here on a large canvas is seen another masterpiece.

From this great, cool, red marble hall we reached some of the private apartments, the arrangements of which reflected the individual and unique taste of the Empress. A balcony from each room gave a superb view of the blue waters and the mountains of Albania towering into the sky.

As there are over a hundred rooms in this vast palace, time would not permit us to inspect them carefully. We were all much struck by the smallness of the rooms, and by the enormous amount of care and forethought which must have been exercised in the arranging of them.

The *salons* were nearly all Empire, very often with black marble walls, black marble fire-places, and furnished in ebony, with heavy black and gold draperies.

There was a completely fitted gymnasium, where the Empress daily went through the most strenuous physical exercises. Next to her simple bedchamber was the famous marble bathroom, where the enormous bath is sunk deep down in the floor, and reached by three marble steps.

Everywhere we looked plainly showed that this Imperial villa, with its stable accommodation for at least forty or fifty horses, must have cost an enormous sum of money.

Our return journey, through the grounds, caused more exclamations of delight. Truly a dream of extraordinary loveliness, which no pen of any writer has ever successfully described.

Fields of roses of the rarest kind, so planted that there are thousands in bloom all the year round, avenues of mimosa, meeting and mingling overhead, orange and citron groves, drooping their perfumed branches, all are arranged so naturally that one forgets that they have been specially cultivated. Many beautiful plants have been brought from the tropics, every kind of lily grows to perfection in that beautiful Grecian climate, and into the warm and scented air myriads of tiny fountains send their refreshing waters to cool this luxuriant vegetation.

Ere we reached the park gates, where the carriages were waiting, we visited the little harbour. This is guarded by a lighthouse, and the Empress's yacht *Miramar* was often anchored there.

"Tante Elizabeth's house is like a fortress," said one of the young Archduchesses. "If there had been a war she could always have seen the soldiers coming, from the terraces and the roof."

"Bravo!" said her father. "Quite surely if the Romans came to fight the Greeks, Achilleion would make an admirable fortress!"

I wonder what the German Emperor, when he

THE INTERIOR OF ACHILLEION, CORFU

paid that big sum of money to acquire this rocky promontory, which so commands the sea and land, would have thought, had he overheard the significant words of the wise little Austrian Princess !

On our return drive to the yacht, through still more enchanting scenes, our attention was often arrested by the various types of Grecian women, either peasants, riding to their homes on donkeys or mules, or of the more educated classes. But all were beautiful—all in picturesque garb.

In none of the many foreign lands of Northern and Southern Europe, which we had travelled with this Imperial Family, were there to be found such really beautiful and stately women as here. The soldiers, too, in their short white skirts, falling so full above their knees, their quaint scarlet zouaves and peculiarly turned up shoes, added to the charm and picturesqueness which surrounded Elizabeth's palace.

On reaching the harbour, the usual crowd awaited our arrival, anxious to see the relatives of the late Empress, and the owners of the great white yacht anchored out at sea.

Archduke Karl Stefan hurried us all into our

several boats, and gave quick directions to the officers in charge, and we were soon rowed across to the *Watūrūs*, already waiting to steam out of harbour.

Arrived on board, the Archduke found a private message had been telegraphed during his absence from the Government authorities, warning him that reports of an alarming character had been received of a possible attack on some member of the Imperial Family, and urging him to take precautions and change the directions of his cruise for the next few days.

This rumour was not generally known on board until the next morning; and by the Archduke himself no notice whatever was taken.

The dinner-hour was fixed for 6.30 that evening, as the beautiful summer day had changed rather suddenly into a stormy evening, and it was thought advisable to retire to our cabins as early as possible.

When the Imperial Family had withdrawn, and most of the suite had retired, I walked to the end of the upper deck, and wondered, as I looked across the dark and stormy waters, whether it would not be much more enjoyable to remain for awhile and revel in the glorious motion of the vessel plunging through the angry waves.

"Are you remaining up on deck, to take part in any possible attack?" suddenly said the mocking voice of Archduke Karl Stefan, as his towering form suddenly appeared before me, in a long dark coat only partly concealing his white naval evening dress. "If so, come along up on the bridge, and I'll get one of the officers to load a rifle."

"I am afraid I am very dense, but I do not quite follow the meaning of Your Imperial Highness's strange remark. It is only nine o'clock, and, as Your Imperial Highness knows, I am particularly fond of a rough sea."

"Yes, yes, I know," interrupted the Archduke, "but it's a fact. I *did* receive warning in Corfu that some idiots were making a dead-set at us. Of course it's all rubbish. Of such rumours I never take the slightest notice; and, now we are out at sea, nothing can happen. There is always more or less of a risk, putting in at these foreign harbours. What is it?" he said hastily, as the first mate on duty stood saluting at his side.

Some unintelligible remarks were passed, and the Archduke swung round, strode along the deck, and ran lightly up the steps leading to the bridge.

I had scarcely begun to think over the Archduke's uncanny remarks, when a shot rang through the air across the deck, from the direction of the coast.

"Quick, Miss," came the shouts from several sailors who were about on the upper deck, and mostly off duty, "get down, quick, off that raised part—on the floor of the deck—or hide behind something."

And in a moment all the men had lain down, or stooped behind some object.

I can remember very distinctly feeling quite unconcerned as I scrambled down on my knees, and popped my head once or twice above the wooden railings, as the shots whizzed past us from what appeared to be, in the darkness, a very old-looking sailing-boat with red sails.

From the bridge, orders came loud and sharp, and in what seemed only a second or two shots were being fired thick and fast by the Archduke and officers around, while the yacht was swung out to sea to the order of " Full steam ahead."

It was a thrilling moment, and only when the danger was well past did one begin to realise what might have been. Next morning, at the breakfast-table, the topic of conversation was how we were chased by brigands along that little bit of Turkish coast.

The Archduke looked across at me, helping himself to Keiller's marmalade—he insisted on English breakfasts always on board yacht.

" I suppose the Miss heard nothing of the fight at sea last night ? "

Knowing the Archduke's delight in trying to make one feel embarrassed, I gave a non-committal reply :

" I think I did hear some firing, Your Imperial Highness, but for what reason I only learnt this morning."

I

CHAPTER XI

THE IMPERIAL CHÂTEAU IN GALICIA

SOON after the war broke out, I heard that Archduke Karl Stefan had sent word that as many as possible of his family should remain altogether in their Polish castle in Galicia.

Frau von Kloss came from Pola, as her husband was called at once to the scene of action on the high seas; and Archduchesses Renata and Mechtildis came from their respective homes. They all remained for a short time with their mother, Archduchess Maria Theresa.

But very soon this beautiful old house, only four or five hours' journey from Cracow, ceased to be a very safe or sheltered haven for an Imperial Family, and the rumour went forth that all had left, and taken up their residence in Vienna.

And Zywiec! An ancestral home of great

ZYWIEC CASTLE, GALICIA.   THE OLD PART

beauty, standing in the midst of a fine old park, and forest lands stretching for miles around, is it possible it no longer exists ?

Has it met the same fate in this terrible war that so many other great and beautiful things have done ?

I have such happy recollections of Zywiec. Archduke Karl Stefan and his family took such enormous pride and pleasure in this glorious old home. Since the time of the famous Archduke Albrecht, to whom it belonged, additions have been made by Archduke Karl Stefan himself, and the Castle is now a unique example of regal splendour—a wonderful triumph of art.

The great stone building is quaint and picturesque, being only two storeys high, and is divided into two parts, generally referred to as the Old Castle and the New Castle.

These are joined at one end by immense stables, and the whole vast building is constructed round an enormous quadrangle.

There is, running almost the entire length of the Castle, a very large stone corridor, on the walls of which are beautiful pictures, and here and there a wide winding staircase leads down into picturesque halls and vestibules, used for dancing, games and all kinds of delightful gatherings.

From this corridor, the various suites of apartments lead off, occupied by the young Archdukes and Archduchesses.

Each one has his or her own set of rooms, consisting of a delightful bedroom, leading out of a study, and a luxurious sitting-room beyond, containing everything that is costly and particularly precious to each individual Imperial child.

In the front part of the Castle are the state rooms, and the private apartments of the Archduke and Archduchess.

There is the famous white and gold *salon*, a vast room, with windows leading on to a terrace, and views across the park and the Tatra Mountains beyond.

On the ground floor are endless delightful reception rooms, leading out of one another, until finally the big ball-room is reached, leading out of a magnificent winter garden.

This then is the favourite residence of the Imperial Family, situated amidst wild and magnificent country, little known to the Englishman.

Hemmed in, as it were, by Silesia, Moravia,

Hungary and Russia, this little bit of Galicia possesses marvellous diversity of life and scenery. Amidst the Carpathian Mountains, there are great fir forests and meadowland, with tiny villages, the inhabitants of which, in their short, full blue skirts, bright red bodices and brilliant head-gear, form charming and picturesque groups.

But working, and always busy—that is the one fact that immediately arrests attention in travelling through any part of this vast Austrian Empire. Every bit of land, whether on hill or plain, is cultivated or made use of by the peasants; and the land is carefully tilled, with a clever scientific knowledge.

At quite a short distance to the north of Zywiec are the world-famed salt mines of Wieliczka. There, too, one is amazed at the industry of these people.

Alas, that vast territory of underground splendour, and the labour of hundreds of years, may now be no more.

It was on December 5th we heard, by a casual war telegram, that the Russians had taken Wieliczka. But what of the white world below?

I remember so well the enormous excitement caused by my visit to the salt mines, after gaining the sanction of Their Imperial Highnesses to join a small party of people who were venturesome enough to descend.

I journeyed to Cracow, that fascinating town, with its wonderful historical past, its interesting people, with their quaint customs and picturesque costumes. Then I made an adventurous journey from Cracow to Wieliczka, in a slow, stuffy train filled with strange and weird Poles ; and an hour's drive in a rough peasant's cart, across wild and desolate country, brought me to the entrance of the salt mines.

There in the offices of the manager I found the party assembled.

We were asked to leave our coats and hats in a room. We were then given extremely picturesque long white cloaks, and tightly fitting head-gear, which I thought admirable—and very necessary, I found later—for the exploration of the dazzling white caves below.

In hydraulic lifts, six at a time, we descended to the first level, about 300 feet below, where we waited until the whole party was assembled.

How very weird it was ! We were given queer-

shaped, swinging lanterns, and in procession we
slowly groped our way along very dark and
endlessly long passages, till we reached the top
of a staircase leading down into the famous
Letow ball-room, where, with one accord, we
all stood breathless, as there burst upon our
view a wonderful world of beauty, scarcely to
be imagined.

Salt, dazzling salt, everywhere salt : chandeliers of salt hung from the roof, from which
flashed hundreds of electric lights ; statues of
salt adorned the walls ; massive pillars, galleries,
quaintly shaped benches and seats, all carved
out of solid rock salt.

At one end was an enormous Austrian eagle,
and in an alcove at the other end stood a throne,
the crystals of which flashed green and ruby
red, and in this the Emperor Franz Josef has
sat on several occasions, when he has presided
over festive gatherings.

As we went slowly down the glittering salt
staircase into this fairy hall, from a great
balcony far above us there burst upon our
ears delightful strains of music from an excellent military band. At the same time
countless fireworks were let off in far-away

corners, and wonderful coloured lights were turned on, so that the whole scene sparkled with a lustre of precious stones; and we, in our quaint costumes, with our swinging lanterns amidst all this fairy-like splendour, felt indeed we were far away from the humdrum world above.

Not a great distance from this gay scene, we came to St. Anthony's Chapel, which dates back to the sixteenth century, and brings us to an entirely different atmosphere, which might almost be considered the religious centre of the salt region. The altar is beautiful, with its many exquisite carvings, all executed in salt.

Many really wonderful statues are seen in the various side chapels and shrines, and over all this hangs one of the most elaborate chandeliers.

From it shine many subdued coloured lights. The music is exquisite, just low, grand and solemn, and one wanted to linger, or sit for awhile in the beautifully carved pews, which have been made down the length of the Chapel.

But there was much more to be seen. I learnt afterwards that the length of the mines

SALT MINES AT WIELICZKA, GALICIA.   THE RESTAURANT AND RAILWAY STATION

is between two and three miles, and there are about seven or eight levels. The most interesting parts of the mines were on the third and fourth levels, most of which we were shown, and down far below the business arrangements of the mines were carried on.

Our little procession descended more steps, many more, until we came to the railway centre, and famous restaurant, where we were very glad to sit at the little tables, rest awhile, partake of the refreshments offered to us, and listen to the delightful tales of our amiable and most attentive guides.

The scene was truly extraordinary, the masses of converging railway lines, the rumble of the trains in the tunnels; the hundreds of lights in the front of the station, and masses of salt around, above and below.

After resting awhile we were taken along the railway lines, through several very long tunnels, to a still greater contrast, namely, a large lake, over which we glided in a most picturesque old barge, once more to the strains of exquisite music.

I suppose we must have been down in this city of salt about three hours, and it was suggested by some that we had been underground long enough. The atmosphere in some of the long passages, and in different parts of the caves, was decidedly damp and chill ; and some of us began to feel the effects of this moist cold air. And so, after traversing more winding tunnels, and ascending many more steps, we reached a lift, which once more took us to the land above.

Before returning to Zywiec I had again the good fortune to spend some time in Cracow, that Polish Kingdom under Austrian rule, where the Pole is so much more free than in the other two Polish Provinces of Russia and Germany.

I made straight for the big central square, or the Ring, where the buildings so vividly recall to one's mind the glorious past of Cracow in its great days.

The two tall towers of St. Mary's Church always attract one's notice at once ; and, if one happens to be there on a feast day, when the great building is crowded to overflowing, and hundreds of poor are content to kneel outside, and all round the church, one is struck by their wonderful religious zeal.

No peasant on any pretext, winter or summer,

would think of missing his Mass ; they come in from the neighbouring villages for miles and miles around—men, women and children.

It is a wonderful sight to look down on this seething mass of humanity engaged in silent prayer, and content to kneel outside a church. The rich colouring of their garments, especially of those of the women, who are very often without shoes and stockings, seems to complete a wonderful picture in this far-off Polish town.

All around are different types of buildings, and all are well and beautifully built. Not far from the Ring is the famous old Castle, with its mighty tower and arches, making a noble pile rising high above the Vistula ; then there are the famous museums and galleries, where are to be seen such priceless works of art.

There are, however, in Galicia many miles of grey and bleak country, where alas, the peasants, especially the Polish peasants, are so poor that they have every appearance of being just wild savages.

The poverty is terrible, and one wonders how it is possible they can exist at all, for indeed in winter the poor things do not live, they just exist. Five or six families will live together in one miserable wooden hut, and their animals with them.

For practically half the year the ground is covered deep in snow, and these wretched beings sleep sometimes for two or three days on end; then they wake to take some kind of meal, which during the winter scarcely ever consists of meat at all.

The conversation of these Polish peasants, in these out-of-the-way poor districts, is absolutely unintelligible; they are practically all half-witted, and their miserable faces, with the long unkempt hair, bear a striking resemblance to the animals with whom they live.

CHAPTER XII

AMUSEMENTS AT ZYWIEC CASTLE

IN and around Cracow several Polish princes and nobles lived in their historic mansions, and from time to time they were invited to spend a few days at Zywiec, or they were asked to join Archduke Karl Stefan at one of his hunting-boxes.

On these occasions, at the Castle, some extra functions were arranged in their honour, besides the daily formal luncheons and dinner parties.

There was sure to be a grand concert specially arranged, which took place in the white and gold *salon*, or in the ball-room if there were many guests invited.

Throughout Austria, music is everywhere of that high standard which commands the reverence and respect of all lovers of music, and that which was heard in the Archduke's palace was always noted for its delicacy and remarkable execution, whether rendered by an orchestra or by a single performer.

The Archduke always performed himself, and the names of many noted players have been given in the same programme, but quite surely it would be difficult to find anyone who could play Chopin with such marvellous power and passionate feeling as Karl Stefan.

One day we had the delight of hearing Kubelik. He was invited to lunch first with the Imperial Family, and great was the excitement of the young Archduchesses to find that he never used a knife, and that his food was cut up by his accompanist, who of course always sat near him at table.

His hands were extraordinarily fragile and beautiful, and he spoke to us of the great fear he always had of any accident happening to them through the use of a knife.

Afterwards in the *salon*, his rapt and marvellous execution won the applause of all. Great too was the delight of the Archduchesses when asked to choose anything they wished to have performed. Certainly his memory was astounding.

I think the early autumn, when the Imperial

Family generally arrived in Zywiec to remain there until going South, was a time greatly enjoyed by all.

The daily drives, picnics and expeditions into the glorious wild country, were an acknowledged delight.

Perhaps an early start would be made ; three or four carriages would be filled by the Imperial party—always attended with a certain amount of ceremony.

The coachmen and footmen, in their resplendent livery, the imposing outriders, always called forth intense excitement on the part of the lonely peasants in the little villages, through which we would drive on our way to some shooting-box, or to some particular pine forest, where we would descend, and then make an exhausting climb up a zigzag and rugged mountainous path. Suddenly at some great height, always in a spot commanding a superb view of the gigantic mountain peaks and rushing torrents below, we would find the Imperial servants who had been sent on some hours before.

There, in that glorious air, with the soft scent of the pines around, a delicious lunch awaited us.

Notwithstanding the enormous height, hot soup, cooked over a crackling wood fire, hot potatoes cooked in the ashes—a favourite Austrian dish—and sausages cooked in the excellent Viennese fashion, besides countless cold delicacies, would be served. All this elaborately prepared meal, for a party of a dozen and more, was a welcome sight when we reached the summit.

But very often in Zywiec there would be days and days of rain, when it would be impossible to leave the Castle. The rain in those parts was terrible, a ceaseless heavy downpour; the rivers and streams would rise, and enormous havoc and destruction would be wrought. After the rain had ceased, the scene in the far-away districts would be dreadful. The angry, rushing torrents would roar and rage past, carrying great trees, bridges, bits of the poor peasants' huts, and one trembled to think of the countless homes that would be wrecked.

All sorts of indoor games would be played in the Castle by grown-ups and young.

If the Archduke happened to be at home, one would be sure that an unusual noise and commotion would arise. A favourite game was

ZYWIEC CASTLE, GALICIA. THE NEW PART

" Railways." An enormous room was set aside for this ; there countless railway lines, stations, signal boxes and all the paraphernalia connected with a great railway would be seen.

The engines and trains were most real, and of course were worked by steam ; each one would be asked to take up a position by some junction or station, and weird and amusing and very deafening scenes would take place.

The greatest joy was if a collision took place, or if anything caught fire.

I think to a stranger looking in to see the Archduke sitting or lying full length on the ground, most serious and attentive to his particular duty, with various ladies and gentlemen, as well as the eager young Archdukes and Archduchesses, the scene would be most unexpected and enlightening.

In late November and December, the country would be covered with snow ; and a heavy frost made the rivers and pieces of water ready for skating.

That was joy indeed. Wheels were removed from every vehicle, of rich and poor, and sleighs with their merry tinkling bells, were the order of the day.

K

Under the bluest of skies, and a brilliant sun, we would sleigh into the snow-covered mountain country, or skate for hours on the beautiful little river in the park.

There again, if the Archduke were present, the games on the ice would be of the wildest, and the scene a joy to behold.

Christmas was always spent in Zywiec; and in no other country are these fête days kept with such wonderful ceremony as in Austria.

For weeks beforehand the preparation began, and to Archduchess Maria Theresa and her lady-in-waiting fell the greatest share of the work—for it certainly was exhausting and most thorough.

When the wishes—which were written down on paper—of the Imperial children had been collected, the lady-in-waiting asked each of the ladies attached to the suite to name two or three of her wishes; and the Lord Chamberlain found out the special desires of the various gentlemen attendants.

The ladies' maids, valets, men and maid-servants, and the outdoor servants were all remembered.

The Archduchess and Countess Huyn then journeyed to Vienna, and several days were passed in making purchases, for, besides all the relatives and the many poor families in whom Her Imperial Highness was interested, no one of her enormous household was ever forgotten.

For several days beforehand, one of the great halls was kept locked, and stupendous preparations went forward.

The great day was Christmas Eve. At about five o'clock every one adjourned to the Chapel, where a beautiful crib had been arranged, and hymns and carols were sung.

The dinner took place at seven o'clock, after which every one assembled in the main entrance hall, and the procession moved forward to the particular staircase that led down into the festive hall.

A veritable fairyland met the eye, and in the centre was a Christmas-tree reaching right up to the lofty ceiling, which was one mass of glittering lights, and hung with beautiful gifts. Round the hall, arranged as in a great bazaar, were tables draped in white cloths, where were set out the presents for each and all of the great assembly, and on each separate table the name of the recipient was printed.

At one side of the hall was a group of servants. One by one they were called up, and the Archduchess presented some suitable and precious gift, on the receipt of which the generally blushing and nervous servant bowed deeply, and kissed the hand of Her Imperial Highness.

The presents of the young Archdukes and Archduchesses were magnificent and costly, but they were always chosen with great care and forethought. It would be impossible to enumerate the presents I have seen given to the Imperial children at the delightful Christmas gatherings I have spent with this family.

I have seen dear little fat ponies led into the hall; there have been wonderful carriages, sleighs, magnificent jewellery. To the members of the suite some beautiful jewel or costly fur was given, besides countless smaller presents.

Great excitement prevailed over the dismantling of the tree, and generally the Archduke contrived that some branch or other should catch fire, to frighten and alarm the entire assembly for the space of a minute.

The life of the party at all the gatherings, up till a few years back, was the gay and delightful Count Chorinsky, who always saw that no one was overlooked.

Then Christmas Day itself was a great feast day. In the morning every one attended Mass in the Chapel, which was beautifully decorated. On leaving the Chapel we all went through the solemn duty of wishing each other " A Happy Christmas." The Archduke and Archduchess stood to receive the good wishes of all, and in turn every one went forward, bowed low and kissed the Archduchess's hand. In the afternoon another Christmas-tree gathering took place for the children of all those employed on the estate. That was a great and joyous event, and every one went and helped to amuse and make merry.

The many, many poor families around were never forgotten by Their Imperial Highnesses, and once again we have brought before us the exceeding kindness and generosity of the Hapsburg family.

At Zywiec Castle dances were a great feature, and, like the majority of Austrians, all the family of Karl Stefan danced extremely well.

Very often from Cracow, or from a small town called Bielitz some distance away, a band was commanded to play in the Castle. Great excitement and preparation reigned, for generally these dances were quite impromptu, and Archduchess Maria Theresa sent round to all of us a little verbal message that in such and such a room, or hall, a ball would take place, and they were nearly always fancy-dress gatherings, with very little time to prepare one's costume.

Nevertheless, as one might rightly imagine, the dresses were always original, and extremely gorgeous ; and the fun was fast and furious, for these gatherings were more or less quite informal, with very few outsiders invited.

Archduke Karl Stefan always wore some comic disguise, in which he was difficult to recognise, though his great height generally gave the secret away.

He always insisted on a country dance being arranged, so that every one might dance at the same time. The Swedish dance was a great favourite, for it gave a splendid opportunity for the various costumes to be examined and criticised, as we all arranged ourselves in lines and couples down the length of the hall. Anyone whose costume was at all eccentric or attractive was sure to derive his or her full share of loud remarks, sometimes very embarrassing remarks.

One little lady had chosen to come one evening dressed as a Polish bride. The costume was correct in every detail, having been lent by a lady of a wealthy Polish family. It was a most tiresome dress to wear, being extremely elaborate, with many short and very full muslin skirts, which appeared to contain dozens of yards of material, and all worn over several stiff and very full petticoats. The shoes were a most peculiar shape, and the head-dress extremely picturesque.

The lady, one of the Austrian governesses, always very shy and nervous, seemed to have attracted the attention of Archduke Karl Stefan, and was teased unmercifully the whole evening. When her turn came to dance down the length of the hall with her partner, and catch the hand of the dancer at the extreme corner, by accident or by some one's mischievous design, she caught her foot half-way down the slippery floor, and fell headlong, disappearing, as it were, in a sea of voluminous skirts and frills.

The Archduke was the first to rush and pick her up out of masses of starched muslin, whilst the entire assembly was convulsed with laughter at the very undignified but comical tumble of the Polish bride.

Very soon after Christmas, preparations were made for leaving Zywiec for the sunny South, with a few gay and delightful days spent on the way at the palace in Vienna.

The preparations, the packing up and the journeys of the entire Imperial Family and entourage were always most exciting.

There was a special train commanded, or special carriages were attached to the night train.

At Zywiec Station the state waiting-room was prepared, red carpet laid on the platform, and all the officials were resplendent and ready with set speeches.

Then again at Vienna, some one representing the Emperor would be at the station to receive us, and again red carpet, with part of the platform partitioned off, and plenty of brilliant uniforms would be seen, and bouquets of

flowers would be presented.   Outside were
always many royal carriages, which are very
imposing equipages, with their coachmen and
footmen in silver and crimson livery.

Once more we would drive through the gay
streets of Vienna, where every moment some
one in resplendent uniform would stand and
salute, as the Imperial carriages passed on the
way to the beautiful palace in the Albrecht
Platz.

CHAPTER XIII

VIENNA, THE GAY CAPITAL

VIENNA! Once the gay capital of the splendid Empire of Austria-Hungary, held together for so many years by the indomitable courage and tenacity of the Emperor Franz Josef.

How is it to-day? Its gaiety is no more, and it looks towards the future with suspense, for a dreadful foreboding is gaining ground that, as the capital of a vast empire of many races and creeds, it has had its day.

And the aged Emperor, whose long life has seen so many personal tragedies, must now look on at the tragic downfall and dismemberment of the Empire that he has striven so zealously to consolidate and aggrandise as the proud heritage of the House of Hapsburg.

I have stayed in Vienna some six or eight times, and the desire to return, and to return

138

SCHÖNBRUNS, THE SUMMER RESIDENCE OF THE EMPEROR OF AUSTRIA

again, is always with me. I think it is much more beautiful even than Paris.

The city has a peculiar charm of its own, and it is unrivalled for the beauty of its surroundings. To obtain one's first glimpse of the gay capital, one should drive in an open fiacre round the Ring, a great wide street, planted with immense trees and gardens, that encircles the entire city.

All the buildings are magnificent, with plenty of space and picturesque gardens between. The luxurious and superb Opera House, the Burg Theatre, St. Stefan's, with its tapering and wonderful spire, and the magnificent *Rathaus* —all these handsome buildings are seen with joy, because of their splendid positions and the amount of space around them.

And then music is again everywhere, in all the parks, in the cafés—joyous, light music, played by military bands, most surely the finest in the world. The streets are at all times gay with the gorgeous colours of the men in uniform, who always struck me as being the smartest and most military-looking men of all the foreign capitals I have visited ; then the dresses of the Viennese women are so chic, so excessively well tailored, that I think in no other country can one see such crowds of really well-dressed women.

"Will you come to the Prater? Countess Huyn has most kindly offered to drive us there this afternoon," said one of the Fräuleins, the first afternoon after our arrival.

It was my first visit to Vienna, and as I was most anxious to squeeze as much as possible into the few days we were to be there—on our way to Pola—I gladly accepted.

It was early spring when I first saw the world-renowned Prater, that long beautiful drive out from the centre of Vienna, with superb gardens and trees on either side, where every type of amusement, fashionable restaurant and famous beer-garden abounds, each rivalling the other with the best of music.

Countess Huyn promised to pick us up in about an hour's time, and drive us back to the palace. Meanwhile we found ourselves comfortable chairs, and prepared to enjoy the endless parade of Viennese wealth and beauty, under the shade of the blossoming chestnut-trees in the Haupt Allee, said to be one of the gayest sights in Europe.

"Now," said my companion with a contented

sigh, " I will try to point out the celebrities. So far you have seen no one in Vienna except Archduchess Valérie, and Archduke Franz Salvator, who lunched at the Palace to-day. You know, of course, she is the Emperor's daughter, and the Archduke is our Archduchess Maria Theresa's brother ? "

" Oh, yes," I said, always delighted to hear anything concerning the complicated relationship of the Austrian Imperial Family, " I have just grasped the fact that the Emperor's daughter is our Archduchess Maria Theresa's sister-in-law. How interesting ! She seems so very kind, simple and unassuming that it is almost impossible to believe that her marriage is so miserable, and that she is epileptic, and perhaps not quite normal—at least that is what one hears in England."

" What utter nonsense and abominable lies ! " burst forth my Austrian informant very excitedly. " Why, it is a most successful and happy marriage ; she is awfully happy, most energetic and always doing something for the people. You English people have a very wrong idea of our Court, they are not by any means all mad and bad. Ah !—there now—look—

that is Archduke Eugene, supposed to be the handsomest man in Vienna; he is our Archduke Karl Stefan's brother; now he is certainly not insane or bad; he belongs to the Imperial Order of Knights, which does not permit him to marry. He is extraordinarily clever, he is Colonel of his Cavalry Regiment, and I think a Doctor of Divinity, and he is very often sent to represent the Emperor at the various foreign courts on the occasion of a wedding or coronation. He is tremendously popular, and the favourite uncle of our Archduchesses; he is so musical that he has his own orchestra."

"Yes," I said, as my eyes followed the handsome dark head of the Archduke as he swung along, in his long white coat over some gorgeous uniform, "he is awfully good-looking, and he must be at least six feet three inches. He seems to know every one, and the women apparently regard him with much favour."

Just then my attention was drawn to one of the brilliant Court carriages, with the coachmen and footmen in their bright and wonderful liveries, coming along at a great pace.

"Now who is this?" said the little Fräulein, standing up to get a good view of the occupants

as they swept past us. " Ah, the carriage is
open—good. Yes, it is the Heir-Apparent and
his morganatic wife, Countess Chotek. Curious
that he is still not very popular; she is very
clever, and is gradually getting herself to the
front. Handsome woman, isn't she ? "

" Indeed she is, and she looks so very regal,
and how happy and contented they both look!"
and I turned to gaze after this much-talked-of
royal couple as they drove by. " Do tell me,
please," I said, turning eagerly to my excited
companion—I had heard already that discussing the different members of the Austrian
Court was the favourite topic of conversation
of this energetic lady—"is Franz Ferdinand any
relation to our Archduke ? I do want to learn
how they are all connected ; I am so hopelessly
bewildered."

" Why, of course, it is most difficult for a
stranger, and more so because they are all so
closely connected. Just ask me anything, and
I'll try to put it right," said my kind informant,
waxing more and more enthusiastic at the idea
of holding forth on her beloved topic to a complete stranger.

" You did not know then that the Heir-

Apparent is first cousin to our Archduchess ?
You see, her mother, Archduchess Immaculata,
and Archduchess Annunciata, mother of Franz
Ferdinand, were sisters. They are extremely
friendly with our family just now, even though
he passed over Karl Stefan's niece in favour of
her lady-in-waiting. Dear me ! there was a
fuss. He used to visit daily at the Palais
Friedrich, and we all expected to hear of one
of the young Archduchesses there marrying our
future Emperor. Really," said Fräulein, with
a funny little shake of her head, " it is wonderful
what a good tonic will do—just look at him for
an example."

" But," I said, laughing and very perplexed,
" what has a good tonic to do with his marrying
Countess Chotek ? "

" Why, everything," she said, " and that is
how she played her cards. At the different
receptions and parties, she used apparently to
take pity on the weary and tired-looking Archduke, of whose health every one had despaired,
and who had repeatedly refused to take the
prescribed remedies.

" They would sit together and she would
listen to his woeful tales, and urge and coax

him to try at least for a time to take the despised
medicine, and really, to cut a long story short,
she induced him so cleverly and put forth all
her most fascinating charms, that he promised
her to take the tonic without fail three times a
day, and when he returned after some months
from his rest cure he was just as you see him
now, strong, healthy and robust-looking."

" How very romantic and amusing. But the
Emperor gave his consent to the marriage
without putting any obstacles forward, did he
not ? I know we were all surprised at the match
in England ! "

" Oh ! indeed, yes, but there *was* a great fuss,
and the secret was first found out by Archduchess
Isabella, who one day discovered a photograph
of the Countess amongst some things which the
Archduke had left to be sent after him. I
believe she was furious with the lady-in-waiting,
and asked her to resign her position ; then the
Emperor got to hear of the attachment, and,
though at first he would not give his consent,
in the end he permitted the marriage."

Our afternoon was already drawing to a close,
and we began to wend our way to the spot
where we had arranged to await the Countess.

L

Several celebrated actresses were pointed out to me, as we slowly walked on through the ever-changing, superbly dressed crowd.

Just at that moment a quiet-looking carriage, drawn by two high-stepping horses, drove past.

" Look," said Fräulein, touching my arm, "that is Frau Schratt ; she is our Emperor's lifelong friend. You will probably have heard many stories connecting their names. Nobody knows the real truth apparently, but she seems to have been a devoted friend, and long before the Empress's death, in the days when she was the famous actress, she was always somewhere near. The Emperor goes to see her constantly even now, and, from what people say, she is always the one who can cheer him up, and she knows how to say the right thing in some of his lonely hours. " Ah, here is Frau Gräfin."

We both got into the carriage, which at that moment drove up. Then the Countess, ever kind and thoughtful, took us to a very famous café in the centre of Vienna, which was filled with a fashionable throng—many of whom the Countess knew personally.

Most certainly my stay at the Austrian Court was rendered very agreeable owing to the great kindness of Countess Natalie Huyn. She was always ready to do her utmost to make my stay pleasant, and often helped me by a timely hint on some matter of etiquette.

The first three or four visits I paid to Vienna, we generally stayed in a part of Archduke Friedrich's palace, which was always in readiness for Archduke Karl Stefan and his family. Now for some years they have had their own palace in Wiednerhaupt Strasse.

This was again another act of prudence and great foresight on the part of Karl Stefan. Until the young Archduchesses were nearly grown up, he kept them away from the gay Court of Vienna, only permitting them to pass a few days there at a time, two or three times a year. He knew the ways of the Court, and, like the late Empress, he thought the kindest and best way of educating and bringing up Imperial children was away from the Court as much as possible, with plenty of healthy change and travel.

Needless to say, the few days' sojourn in Vienna, at the Palais Friedrich, situated in the heart of the city, almost opposite to the famous Opera House, and later on at their own palace in the Wiednerhaupt Strasse, were days of excitement and delight.

A great many visits took place between the different Imperial Families; luncheon and dinner parties were given; and visits to the Opera and theatre were occasionally made by the two elder Archduchesses.

The palace was enormous, most gorgeous and luxurious inside, and I never even went all over it. The part occupied by our Imperial Family was long and rambling, and connected with the greater and still more imposing part occupied by Archduke Friedrich by a covered-in glass corridor, which was really a small bridge passing over the roadway, connecting the two portions of the building. It was possible, which we often did, to walk on through endlessly long halls and wide corridors, to the famous Augustine Chapel, and to the Emperor's palace beyond.

On Sundays and feast days in Vienna, we always assembled in one of the large *salons*, and then walked in procession through the two parts of the immense palace, to hear Mass in the Augustine Church from the private boxes of the Emperor, which were built high up in the wall, and communicated with the palace by a doorway. They were luxuriously roomy and comfortable boxes, but it always struck one as being a curious proceeding to be hearing Mass behind a glass screen, and high up in the walls of a great public church.

I had a delightful suite of rooms in Vienna, consisting of a little ante-room, a charming boudoir and bedroom all communicating, with enormous windows looking down in the private grounds of the Emperor.

These rooms were in a very far-away part of the building, and I remember, during my first visit, I spent many anxious moments wandering along endless corridors in search of my apartments.

I was waited upon by a very elderly maid, who looked after the rooms generally, and bustled about with many large jingling keys. She came to me at the unearthly hour of five o'clock in the morning, and made up three huge fires. She was always most careful to lock the doors, and to lock me in at night. I objected at first very strongly to this, but either my limited German was unintelligible or she did not think it correct or safe. With much shaking of the head, and many gesticulations, she always went away at night, very carefully locking the outer door, after kissing my hand, and murmuring many polite and incoherent speeches.

I found it very irksome and unnecessary; but as she always seemed to be about during the day, and until late at night, I soon became accustomed to the sound of her jingling keys. My other attendant was most kind and attentive too, she was always ready to brush and arrange my dresses, and seemed most anxious to give me any information I cared to ask.

How often I contrasted the education of the Austrians with that of the English!

During my first year I encountered countless difficulties, not being able to converse fluently in German. I scarcely ever met an Austrian woman who was not able to speak with perfect ease and fluency in German, French and English. At the same time an Austrian woman has a complete knowledge of all domestic matters; she is an excellent cook, a brilliant conversationalist, always very witty, and is generally capable of performing on the piano with masterly skill.

I was much impressed one day at the thoroughness of their knowledge and accomplishments.

It was at the house of a well-known Viennese lady and her family, with whom I was dining, and there were present several guests. Before the meal our hostess had been delighting our ears with some most difficult classical music, which one seldom hears performed by an amateur, after which she had sung one of Schubert's love songs with a perfectly trained and charming voice.

At dinner the conversation, always led by her, was both witty and clever, and she was in the midst of discussing Rossetti's powers as a painter and a poet, when one of the servants came to say, in agitated tones, that the cook had slipped and apparently broken his arm. She rose hurriedly from the table, motioned to her daughter to take her place, and begged us all to continue our meal as far as it was possible.

In a surprisingly short space of time our hostess had returned, having temporarily bandaged up the cook's arm, sent for a doctor, and herself cooked a delicious omelette, made the salad, and ordered various cold delicacies to be served. We finished the meal thus—

with coffee made in the *salon* by the hostess herself.

We went on afterwards to a bridge party, and I learnt later it was two days before my friend succeeded in securing a new cook.

Meanwhile she herself cooked for a family of five, and the Viennese are not content with cold meat and boiled potatoes! Their meals are the result of art and skill and much thought.

CHAPTER XIV

LIFE AT THE VIENNESE COURT

THE average Austrian is always gay, light-hearted and generous, and takes nothing seriously except his religion. That becomes more or less a duty and a habit. He rarely misses his Mass, no matter how the rest of his day or night may be spent.

I remember, one Sunday morning, having this fact very clearly impressed upon my mind whilst standing in the crowd in the beautiful St. Stefan's Church—one often stands through a service, there being only a limited number of seats. Presently there passed in front of me the tall and handsome figure of the notorious Archduke Otto, with his aide-de-camp.

He stood through the Mass, a little to the right of me, and directly after it was finished he strode out through the crowd, followed by his companion.

" Now he is off to the house of his latest,

Mademoïselle X——," said my friend. "He will probably spend the rest of the day with her, and probably the night. You remember they were speaking of him at dinner last night. The Court tries to hush up his last drunken debauch, when he invited his favourite companions to visit his wife at her country house, at three o'clock in the morning.

"They all entered the house, and made for her private apartments; she was in bed, of course, and most terribly alarmed and frightened at the commotion and noise. Luckily, one of the men was sufficiently sober to prevent matters going too far; he drew his sword, and protected the Archduchess until help arrived."

"How horrible!" I exclaimed. "And he has just stood through this Mass, so calm and dignified. I have never seen such a fine-looking man, and he certainly does not look like a drunkard."

During my stay in Austria, I several times met this much-talked-of Archduke, and he seemed to be one of the most delightful and fascinating of all the Austrian Princes; but I am forced to admit that he was certainly one

of those Hapsburgs with whose names endless
scandalous stories have been rightly connected.

His career was extraordinary, and he died
some years ago of a most hideous disease,
contracted in the East whilst wandering there
for fresh diversions. His wife, the long-suffering
Marie Josepha, sister of the King of Saxony,
was sufficiently noble and generous to allow
him to be brought to her home, and she nursed
him to the end of his lingering death, the agony
of which lasted nearly a year.

His end was ghastly; all parts of his once
handsome face fell away, as they were gradually
eaten up by the foul disease which one can
rightly judge was the result of his dissipated
life. He was the stepson of the Duchess of
Parma's sister, Archduchess Annunciata, and
his brother was the Heir-Apparent who was
murdered last year.

It is not very hopeful for Austria's future
Emperor, if hereditary failings count, for Arch-
duke Otto's son is the present heir to the throne,
Archduke Karl Franz Josef. One saw him
here in England at the Coronation of King
George, when he came to represent the Emperor.

Karl Franz Josef was born in 1889, and

married Princess Zita, one of the twenty-one children of Duke Robert of Parma, which one might almost venture to say seems a risky choice, as one or two of these children are said to be of feeble and failing intellect.

So far this young couple have led very quiet and uneventful lives, and the few years of their married life have been quite happy and peaceful. Their little son, Franz Josef Otto, is about three years of age; he is so far very strong and healthy, and is idolised by the old Emperor.

Archduke Karl has been very carefully brought up, and his mother, Archduchess Marie Josepha, has been untiring in her devotion and care to the son whose father gave no heed, or good example, to him. She sent Karl for a time to be educated at Stonyhurst College, Lancashire. I heard from time to time, from some friends of mine there, that he thoroughly enjoyed the life, and was most popular.

In Vienna, I sometimes saw him too. He often came to see Archduke Karl, son of Karl Stefan, a very great friend of his, and about his own age.

Again was brought home to me the deeply

religious side of the Austrian people, when I witnessed for the first time that wonderful and impressive procession on the feast of Corpus Christi.

This particular feast is the greatest fête day in the year, and I remember so well the religious pageant, which I was privileged to see from one of the windows at the extreme wing of the Palais Friedrich.

I was awakened one glorious morning in June, at the early hour of five o'clock, by the heavy tramping of the various regiments, as they marched past on their way to the different positions they were to occupy.

Every little while a splendid military band went swinging past, and after Mass in the Augustine Church, where we sat in one of the Imperial boxes of the Emperor, we were conducted by two of the gorgeous Court flunkeys, through endless corridors and rooms, to a great window overlooking the street, in another part of the palace.

The entire route of the procession was lined with soldiers, and at six different parts of the town most beautiful altars were arranged, each under a gorgeous canopy of crimson and gold.

Opposite to each altar a great gold chair was placed for the Emperor, and at a little distance behind gold and crimson chairs were placed for the various members of the Imperial Court. Exactly opposite to our window was one of these altars, so we were very fortunate in being able to see the entire ceremony.

The procession was gorgeous and imposing; and, unless one has actually beheld this religious scene, it is impossible to realise the solemnity and magnificence of it all. It took from eight o'clock until eleven o'clock for the procession to walk over the prescribed route, and all that while the aged Emperor walked alone and bare-headed immediately after the Blessed Sacrament.

First of all there were the priests, who walked in twos, from every church in Vienna, Franciscans, Carmelites, Dominicans, all in their quaint habits; then followed representatives of the Parliament, high officials occupying various positions under the Crown, and the Government, all in their official robes.

The Blessed Sacrament was carried by one of the highest dignitaries of the Church. Then followed the Emperor, walking so splendidly upright in his blue and white uniform, with numbers of page boys in scarlet, gold and white ; and after him came the Archdukes. To see them all together, in their gorgeous uniforms in one vast crowd, was indeed a superb spectacle.

The servants of the Imperial household, and the various aides-de-camp of the Archdukes, were in attendance ; this is a compulsory duty.

As the procession approached each altar, the band, stationed at one side, played the National Anthem.

The Blessed Sacrament was placed on the altar, and the Emperor and Archdukes took up their respective positions, after which they all solemnly and silently knelt.

After a short pause the procession moved slowly on, and more soldiers and officers, and Hungarian Guards on horseback, brought the great and imposing spectacle to an end.

The crowd was immense, wonderful and silent, and again one was impressed at the weary and aged Emperor keeping up this yearly custom, and insisting on the entire religious ceremony being carried out in its exact details.

Then, in a gorgeous white and gold state

coach, drawn by eight cream horses, the Emperor was driven back to the palace. He went at once to the great draped window, where various relatives had been viewing the ceremony, and where he could look down on the seething crowd below who had waited to get yet another glimpse of their beloved monarch.

The Archdukes drove back to the palace in black and gold carriages, drawn by six horses; and some of them were invited to lunch with the Emperor.

Another great, but entirely different occasion, on which I saw practically all the members of the Austrian Court together, was at the Hofburg, on the occasion of the golden wedding of the much-beloved Archduke Rainer, one of the Emperor's favourite cousins, and the first Archduke of the realm.

The celebration of the golden wedding of this Archducal pair attracted enormous sympathetic notice throughout Austria, and especially in Vienna, where they were immensely popular All kinds of festivities, dinners and gala performances were given, and the Emperor and members of the Court called early in the day to offer them congratulations.

A great banquet was given at the Hofburg, and those attached to the various suites of the Imperial Families were presented with cards of invitation to the Hofburg, to witness the procession of royalties entering the banqueting hall.

The Emperor, the Archdukes and Archduchesses, and the various distinguished foreign guests, including Prince and Princess Campofranco and the Infanta Isabella of Spain, met the Archducal pair in one of the great reception halls. Then, walking in couples, with the young children of the Viennese Court going first, a great procession was formed, and this brilliant and distinguished assemblage passed to the royal chapel through the countless gorgeous state rooms of the Hofburg, lined on either side with the imposing Imperial Guards.

The ladies of the Court wore their most beautiful jewels; and their dresses were magnificent beyond description. The superb and picturesque uniforms worn by the men made this glittering assembly for me, at least, a never-to-be-forgotten feast for the eye.

The old Emperor walked so splendidly upright, a forlorn and remarkable figure, quite

M

alone, with no woman to lead by the hand, at the end of the procession, immediately behind the old Archduke and Archduchess Rainer.

Here was yet another example of a much-esteemed and happily wedded Hapsburg; and from every source I could hear of nothing but love and esteem for this wonderful old pair.

The next evening many of us went to the Opera, without doubt the finest in the world.

The house itself is magnificent, with its luxurious vestibule, where is seen the famous imposing staircase. The vast auditorium is excellently planned, and from all seats one can see and hear perfectly.

" Lohengrin " was the first of many operas I heard in Vienna, and I was tremendously impressed with the most perfect way in which they were rendered. The orchestra was the largest in the world, and I heard afterwards that each man must have held a scholarship from the *Conservatoire*. One can judge how superbly they work together, when one understands that they perform practically the entire year at the Opera House in Vienna, and are never heard anywhere else. It is, of course, the same with the singers in the great chorus, and the actors and actresses seen and heard at the Opera are the most famous in the world of music.

Being an institution maintained by the Crown, nothing that money can do is spared in the productions. The repertoire is extensive, and I have often heard operas by Saint-Saëns, Verdi, Gounod, and Rossini as well as those by Wagner.

Although the brilliant uniforms, seen all over the house, and the dresses and jewels of royalty and some of the Viennese aristocracy—when they were present—gave a more or less festive air, I always felt bound to contrast the Viennese audience with that of our own shabby and badly built Covent Garden.

Certainly our London audience stands first in the world for its imposing show of jewels, dresses and opera wraps.

The audience in the Vienna Opera House is distinctly less imposing and magnificent.

I remember my astonishment when walking into the orchestra stalls in Vienna, at being obliged to go back and leave my cloak in a very draughty and badly arranged cloak-room. I was afterwards informed that cloaks are not permitted at the Opera or theatres, and that ladies are not obliged to wear evening dress, and very seldom do so.

The men, too, who are not of the military world are not commanded to don the regulation evening dress, which we English are accustomed to see, so that on entering the vast and magnificent Opera House in Vienna, one cannot help being struck by the lack of the display of beautiful dresses and jewels which makes the audience at Covent Garden the best dressed in the world.

CHAPTER XV

LIFE ON THE IMPERIAL YACHT

OF all the Archdukes at the Court of Vienna, Karl Stefan stands out foremost in his great passion for the sea. No other Austrian Prince has had such a wide experience of life at sea, or has owned such a number of costly and magnificent yachts.

Nearly every year a new one was designed and ordered, and very often an English firm had the honour of building this favourite plaything of Archduke Karl Stefan.

One of the largest and most sumptuous steam-yachts was the *Watūrūs*, built in Leith from the designs of Alfred Brown, a naval architect in London.

The sleeping cabins and bath-rooms were placed on the lower deck, and there was accommodation for over twenty guests, besides ample room for a crew of thirty-five men.

On the main deck were two large drawing-rooms, a dining-room, and two delightful read-ing-rooms; and the vessel throughout was furnished and upholstered in exquisite fashion by Maple. She carried five large boats, and a very powerful steam-launch.

Many were the delightful voyages made on this particular yacht to Spain, Greece, Turkey, Russia, Sweden and other foreign lands.

Great was the excitement when a new yacht was complete, and particularly so when news arrived at Lussin that at last the *Waturus* had made a satisfactory trial journey down the Firth of Forth, with Commander L. von Sztranyavszky, Austrian Attaché in London, and other distinguished people on board.

Archduke Karl Stefan started for Scotland, with Captain Harra, to bring the yacht across to Kiel, where the rest of the Imperial Family and suite were to meet him at the beginning of July.

Our stay in Lussin that particular year was much later than usual, owing to some delay in the finishing of the new yacht; and it was the beginning of June before we left the island for Fiume *en route* for Vienna, where a week's stay was made for final necessary purchases for a three months' cruise.

Whilst there news arrived from the Archduke that a still further delay would be necessary before a start could be made ; and, as Vienna was much too hot in which to linger at that time of year, Count Chorinsky, ever ready with delightful plans and suggestions, advised Archduchess Maria Theresa to spend the next two or three weeks in the north of Germany, where it would be considerably cooler, and at the same time allow the young Princes and Princesses to see fresh scenes.

We were all delighted at this idea, and, after leaving Vienna one glorious summer night in a special train, we arrived at Dresden the next morning at eight o'clock, in time for a delicious breakfast. Leipzig too was a delight to see, although the visit was a short one.

Early one evening we arrived at Hamburg Station, where a great reception awaited us. After the usual ceremonies, speeches and presentations had taken place, we drove in the five carriages, which awaited us, to the palatial and magnificent *Hamburger Hof*, where the entire suite of rooms on the first floor had been reserved for the Imperial party.

The hotel looked on to the great lakes and

the beautiful Jungfernstieg Strasse, and a delightful three weeks was spent at this hotel, where every attention was lavished on the Imperial party, although the Archduchess was travelling incognita under the name of Countess Saybusch.

The German Emperor at once sent Prince Henry of Prussia to welcome them to his land, and the next evening a great dinner was given at the hotel, at which Prince Henry was the guest of honour.

I was presented to this popular Prince in the big *salon*, before we descended in ceremonious fashion down the grand staircase to the big dining-hall.

He spoke, of course, excellent English, and I was at once impressed with his charm and his genial manners. All during dinner he delighted every one with the most amusing stories and anecdotes, and one could not help comparing this jovial sailor Prince with his brother, the Kaiser.

Our meals were always taken in the big public dining-hall, at tables arranged at the extreme end of that immense room.

During our stay the hotel was crowded with

very distinguished foreign and American visitors,
therefore the Imperial party, which consisted
of fifteen, was always a source of much interest
and attention. Besides Archduchess Maria
Theresa and her *dame d'honneur*, Countess
Natalie Huyn, there were the Archduchesses,
Eleonore, Renata and Mechtildis, and the three
Archdukes, Karl, Leo and Willi, attended by
Count Chorinsky, Dr. Krumboldt, Captain Lyst ;
Mademoiselle Seifert, Fräulein von Baender and
Fräulein Wienke. By express order of the
Archduke, every one was supposed to wait
upon himself or herself as much as possible, so
that we had with us not more than three or four
ladies' maids and valets.

Many delightful days were spent sightseeing
in and around Hamburg ; daily boating expeditions were made on the great lakes, and all
along the beautiful river Elbe.

At last one morning a special saloon train
took us all from Hamburg to Brünsbuttel,
where, as we drew up alongside of the red-
carpeted station, the Archduke and all the
crew of the *Watürüs* awaited us. Besides the
station officials, in their smart uniforms and
white gloves, several ladies with bouquets of

flowers were grouped at one end of the station, and in the distance, at the entrance of the famous Kaiser Wilhelm Canal, the great white yacht, gaily decked with flags, could be seen.

After the presentations and various speeches had taken place, we at once went on board the *Waturus*, and the Archduke with great pride and immense satisfaction insisted on the entire party's making a tour of the vessel, and being shown our various apartments by himself.

A chorus of delight and admiration came from all, as we wended our way over the spacious decks, on which two most comfortable and splendidly furnished deck-houses were provided for wet weather. Down a broad staircase we reached an elegant dining-saloon, upholstered in dark green leather, with walls of oak panelling, leading out of which were two light and airy drawing-rooms, with dainty chintzes. Quaint but comfortable seats were let into the wall, piled with soft cushions, and there was everything that money could buy.

The ladies' cabins, all together in the front part of the vessel, were exactly alike, and each one had a separate apartment. They were carpeted in deep red velvet pile, with lounges and cushions, bedspreads and hangings in exquisite old-world chintz. There were elegant wardrobes, with long mirrors, dressing-tables, chests of drawers and wash-stands made in beautiful light oak. Although one so often hears of the cramped discomfort of long voyages at sea, never during the weeks and months spent travelling on any of the Archduke's yachts did one experience anything but the greatest luxury, comfort, and as much space as one could possibly desire.

But the Archduke was excessively particular, and sometimes very fussy over his yacht ; from time to time he would enforce very strict and sometimes rather strange rules.

For example, when we all first arrived on board, he gave out that no trunks were to be taken down the staircase, or into any of the cabins ; all unpacking was to take place on the lower deck. This caused immense inconvenience, and a great deal of annoyance to some, but, if one felt inclined to look on the comic side, the scene which followed was really funny.

Fortunately, on our arrival it was beautifully fine, but I remember on leaving the yacht at the end of our journey it was pouring with rain ; the process of packing was in that case most tiresome and laborious.

One can picture the scene : innumerable, immense open trunks on deck ; maids, valets, sailors, in fact all of us, carrying piles of clothes along the decks, and down the staircases, through several saloons, and another staircase to our respective rooms. By the time the dressing-bell rang, every one was exhausted, and almost ready to collapse with heat and fatigue.

We were all asked to wear white as much as possible ; and on no account to appear on any of the spotless decks other than with india-rubber soles and heels to our shoes or boots.

For some weeks, too, the Archduke decided that tea was a quite unnecessary meal and gave useless work to the servants. Consequently, we had nothing to eat from twelve o'clock luncheon until seven o'clock dinner, and that delightful meal, which one is so accustomed to have about four o'clock, even in Austria, was abandoned.

Archduchess Maria Theresa seemed powerless to alter this strange rule, and for the young Archduchesses it was certainly too long a time to pass—I believe, after many discussions, they

were allowed one orange each at the hour of
four o'clock.

Another rule, about which the Archduke was
most particular, was that whilst the yacht was
in motion no windows or port-holes, under any
pretext whatsoever, were to be opened. To a
certain extent this rule was quite sensible,
except on calm days, when it seemed impossible
that the water could ever enter the windows.
Sometimes, when we made no stop for several
days, the atmosphere in our cabins became very
stifling.

I am afraid I must confess to being very
heedless, and in this instance much too venturesome, for I always opened my porthole whilst in
my sleeping apartment. I took care, of course,
to fasten it on leaving my room.

One night about half-past nine, when we were
in the Baltic, Count Chorinsky came hurrying
to me on deck, where I was sitting in a great
comfortable chair, enjoying a heavenly night
with a high sea running.

"Oh, Miladi," said the Count in his delightful mocking and teasing voice, though this time
he appeared more serious than usual, "the ship
is sinking, your cabin is already under water,

and the waves are pouring in your window!
His Imperial Highness is filled with wrath and
indignation, and you are requested to proceed
at once to your cabin."

At first I thought it was all a joke, then I
remembered the great rule, and the fact that
while dressing for dinner I had opened my port-
hole!

I leapt to my feet and rushed down to my
cabin; the scene which met my eyes, though
not so alarming as painted by the Count, was
truly very bad. As I reached the last stair, the
Archduke, in his pyjamas, was fortunately just
disappearing—I had heard he had retired to
rest, so as to take on some of the night duty on
the bridge—but my door was open, and in the
corridor was piled bedding, blankets and the
beautiful velvet carpet, all soaked with water.
Several sailors were on their knees, with pails,
mopping up the water, and my pretty room was
a scene of desolation.

It seems that, although I had really fastened
my window, I must have failed to secure the
catch sufficiently fast, and the force of the
rough waves had burst it open.

I was filled with chagrin and repentance, and

more so the next morning when I went up on deck before breakfast and saw hanging up to dry, over a line by the beautiful white sails, blankets and bedding, my eiderdown, carpets and an array of various draperies, which told the tale of the mishap to all the world.

I dreaded descending to breakfast, where I felt too well I should be, and quite justly, the subject of the Archduke's righteous anger. All through the meal, happily, no mention was made of the unpleasant subject; but after the repast was over, I thought it would be wiser for me to approach the Archduke and tender my apologies.

I remember that several of the others on board had rather gloated over the adventure, and were quite prepared to rejoice at the prospect of my being no longer in the very good books of the Archduke.

But I came off very well; and, beyond pointing out the fact that my carelessness might have led to a very nasty accident, His Imperial Highness passed the matter over quite lightly with a few laughing remarks.

We left Brünsbuttel the morning after our arrival, and sailed down the wonderful Kaiser

Wilhelm Canal, which has become of such importance in this great European War.

We were all immensely struck by the marvellous construction of this vast work, the bridges across the canal being magnificent, and built with remarkable skill.

At the end of the canal, before entering Kiel Harbour, a short halt had to be made for certain formalities to be gone through, and there a telegram was handed in to the Archduke from his sister, Queen Christina of Spain, wishing him luck on the maiden trip of the *Waturus*.

Kiel Harbour was a superb sight, as we slowly entered and dropped anchor amidst the warships of Germany, and indeed of many other European lands.

All around, too, was every kind of craft from the great racing world, for it was the week of the Kiel Regatta.

As we dropped anchor, salutes were fired, the ships around ran up their flags, and from a German man-of-war quite near to us the sailors lined up on deck, while the Austrian national hymn was played by a splendid military band.

After a very little while steam-launches came puffing up to the yacht, and various distin-

guished callers came on board to welcome the
Imperial Family.   One of the first was Prince
Henry of Prussia, who was anchored a very
little way off in his great racing yacht.   He was
a great friend of Karl Stefan, for they had many
tastes in common.   Prince Henry made an
exhaustive tour of all parts of the yacht, and
was genuinely charmed with the whole arrangement.   The next evening he came to dinner
with Princess Henry, who was perfectly delightful, too.   She is the sister of the Empress
of Russia.

We left Kiel about four o'clock one morning,
after five most enjoyable days spent in watching
the races, and in making excursions on land.
We sailed right up the Baltic Sea to Petrograd without any further halts, except at
Kronstadt for business purposes—a distance of
seven or eight hundred miles.

After a very stormy passage all along the
Baltic, we arrived one Sunday morning in the
harbour of Kronstadt, where a stay of nearly
two hours had to be made, whilst two very particular and important Russian officials came on
board to inspect the passports, papers and cer-
tificates, and to ask endless and searching

N

questions concerning each and every one on board.

I had no passport. That caused a great delay, and the idea of my being allowed to enter Russian territory would certainly not have been permitted, had I not been travelling as one of the suite of an Imperial Highness.

Already one felt the nearness of Russia, and immediately one began to think of the many stories one had heard concerning the terrible Russian spies and their intrigues. The very first batch of letters which were handed to us on board had all been opened, and read by order of the suspicious Russian Police.

CHAPTER XVI

THE RUSSIAN CAPITAL

AFTER the official inspection of the yacht *Waturus*, by the Russian police in the busy and interesting harbour of Kronstadt, in a very short time we were in sight of Petrograd, with its magnificent golden turrets and towers, and its numerous spires and steeples.

In summer the entrance by water to this great Russian capital is truly remarkable, and it is certainly one of the most imposing of all the European capitals. A long and extremely wide canal, with grand old trees, shrubs and exquisite flowers on either side of its picturesque banks, marks the entrance to this majestic town.

We dropped anchor on the river Neva, not very far from the Winter Palace of the Czar.

Immediately after lunch it was necessary for every one to lie down, as the heat in Petrograd at the beginning of August is intense.

179

Between four and five o'clock, our first expedition on Russian territory was made. Two or three of the small boats were lowered, and very swiftly we were rowed across the Neva to the opposite bank, which just there was immensely wide. There four of the most delightful little low carriages awaited us, the famous Russian droshky, drawn by two or three of the fleetest horses, and driven by those grotesque Russian coachmen, with their long flowing brown robes reaching to their feet.

One is astonished at the sight of these peculiar coachmen, on all the cabs and carriages. It is their custom to pad themselves out to the largest dimensions possible, and over all this padding a long flowing robe, secured round the immense waist by a girdle, is worn. They always wear dark, very greasy wigs, with long curls, upon which is set a rather tall, shiny hat. They look very odd, but no one in Petrograd would entertain the idea for one moment of being driven by a lean coachman : they must be so many inches round the waist, and during all seasons they appear to wear just as many clothes. In winter they don a fur cap, fur boots, and many of them wear fur upon their robes.

A RUSSIAN COACHMAN

There are many curious reasons given to explain this peculiar Russian custom. Catherine the Great is said to have insisted that there should always be a certain number of inches between the tip of her nose and the body of her coachman.

Mention has often been made of the rapid driving in Russia, but until you have sat in a droshky, and have been driven by one of those weird coachmen down the principal wide thoroughfare—the Nevsky Prospect—it is impossible to believe the rapidity and the extraordinary skill with which you are whirled through the traffic, at a breathless speed, by these most expert drivers.

The road is so wide, that at least four or five rows of traffic can easily drive along without coming to grief; but you must literally hold on to your neighbour and to the sides of the vehicle, so unexpectedly rapid is the rate with which you are rushed through the streets. You do not easily forget your first drive on Russian soil.

The capital itself is like no other European city. It is on such a colossal scale, with its immensely wide streets and magnificent churches, the richness and gorgeousness of which are well-nigh impossible to describe. The buildings in the streets are all of different-coloured stone, and they stand out to perfection against the superb Northern sky.

Almost immediately one is struck by the deeply religious feeling of the Russians, and on all sides—whether in the streets of a town, or out in a little hamlet in the country—one sees the *ikon*, which is a sacred representation, generally of the Virgin and the Holy Child, whose garments are often adorned with precious stones and jewels, and before which a little lamp is hung.

No one, rich or poor, passes the *ikon* without making either the sign of the cross, or a salutation, whether it is a man, woman, or child, and one quickly learns why the term " Holy Russia " is applied to that surprising land, a land of a few great towns, but of an incredibly vast number of hamlets and villages.

I saw Petrograd for the first time under a blazing sun, during one of its few summer months, when the heat is tropical, and there is much dust, and many mosquitoes.

During these months most of the great

Russian nobles and aristocracy are away in their country houses, which are generally built of wood, with wide balconies and terraces round them. Everywhere one sees signs of enormous wealth and luxury, and foreigners, especially the English, are always most hospitably received. Any hour of the day one is welcome. Visits do not last the formal fifteen minutes, and conversation is not frigid and tiresome.

If the hostess is not at home, there is always some other member of the family to receive visitors with open arms, and one is immediately taken into the family circle in the friendliest manner possible. Tea is at once offered, which is served in various ways, but always very hot and of a light colour.

In the houses of the nobles it is often served with cognac or lemon, and generally in tall glasses with elaborate silver handles. In some households, cups are now being used, but in the restaurants, cafés, and houses of the lower classes, the tea is drunk out of glasses, generally without lemon, and made extremely weak.

One receives many pressing invitations to lunch and dinner, and the impression that one is really welcome is made manifest by the courteous attention of the host and hostess.

The Russian appetiser, or *zakuska*, which precedes the meal, is a great feature of the Russian household. It is often so elaborate and generous that it is sometimes difficult to do any justice to the many courses which follow. Caviare, *pâté de foie gras*, all kinds of skilfully prepared fish, and vodka are the principal items of the *zakuska*.

At the end of a Russian repast, the men and children, if there are any present, go up to the hostess, kiss her hand and thank her in truly courtly fashion. It is a charming custom and makes a great impression on the English visitor.

In the well-to-do families, especially during the last few years, there is always an English governess, or nurse, so that the English language is now very general, and the children begin to speak it from an early age. French, of course, is still the language of society, as it were, and shopping in Petrograd or any other town need not be a difficulty because one is unacquainted with the Russian tongue.

The Imperial Family stayed some time in Petrograd, when as much as possible of the town itself was seen, which, by the way, is a very different place in summer from the Petrograd under winter skies and heavy snow. But Petrograd in winter, when the season is in full swing! To drive out at night into the vast spaces beyond, under a full moon, in a Russian sledge, behind three of those shaggy Russian ponies, with no sounds but the jingling of the bells and the occasional crack of the whip, that, indeed, is to realise the joy of life! One feels a hundred leagues away, and on the edge of the unknown; and, as one is swept through the still snow-laden atmosphere for miles and miles, every now and again, in the far-off distance, the awful stillness will be broken by the cry of some animal.

The Nevski in winter is a sight to remember. All the droshkys are on runners and glide silently along, keeping near the edge of the pavement; the private sleighs and carriages, elaborately carved and decorated, dash along down the centre of the broad thoroughfare. On the pavement one sees every type of fashionable men and women, officers in their brilliant uniform, Cossacks in their astrakhan caps and resplendent attire, galloping past on horseback.

One is seldom in bed before three or four in the morning ; consequently it is often already noon before an appearance is made next day. Then follow luncheons, skating parties, sledge drives, receptions, dinners and dances far into the night.

In winter the houses of the great nobles are heated throughout, and the lightest of clothing can be worn. Outside one seldom feels the cold, because one is wrapped in fur from head to foot. Fur caps and fur boots are always worn, and men in the country wear suits of fur and skins. Every mansion is a veritable palace where one sees on every side sumptuous wealth, the greatest comfort and everything that is artistic.

At a reception or a ball the dresses of the Russian women, superb creations which only Paris or Vienna can produce ; the display of jewels, almost barbaric in their blazing splendour ; the men, Cossacks in red and silver, Hussars and Lancers, men in Court attire, with their orders flashing with precious stones—all help to create a scene with a background of wealth such as is seen in no other European capital.

During that summer, we visited the Winter

PETERHOF, THE SUMMER PALACE OF THE CZAR OF RUSSIA

Palace and Peterhof, then one of the summer residences of the Czar and Czarina. During the last few years, however, the shores of the Crimea have been visited annually by the Russian Imperial Family, because that particular climate seems to have benefited the little Czarevitch in his delicate state of health.

The famous Winter Palace, situated on the Neva, is a vast, magnificent pile, whose very walls, as one enters, seem to vibrate with the costliness and luxury of its many halls, galleries and chambers. It is literally filled with treasures of immense worth; and its reception rooms, leading out of a superb winter garden, are a blaze of gold, precious stones and priceless works of art. Perhaps the most gorgeous of all is the great centre hall, with its many huge windows looking on to the Neva. When lit up by thousands of electric lights, the dazzling splendour of the superb carved ceiling, the gold and precious stones in the walls, and the exquisite inlaid floor are revealed to perfection. From this vast hall one wanders into a winter garden where the rarest of tropical plants are grown, and exquisite statuary is seen amidst curiously contrived fountains whose waters fall melodiously upon one's ears.

Peterhof, some distance away, which we reached by steamer, might almost be spoken of as a dream palace, with a most exquisite situation, its beautiful gardens with their thousands of fountains playing in every conceivable and unexpected corner.

In the grounds are the famous house of Peter the Great and the wonderful bath-house of Queen Catherine, where, besides the great and extraordinarily built bath, sprays of water and fountains, at the touch of a button, spring forth from the floors, walls and ceilings, and from under the seats. The rooms in Peterhof are exquisite and dainty, and they all lead out of one another.

Each chamber has a scheme of colouring. One room is pale blue: pale blue brocaded walls and ceilings, exquisite draperies in pale blue silk, with furniture to correspond, and over a shining floor exquisite rugs in pale blue. Other rooms are white, rose, purple, gold, and one great reception hall has walls of rare old crystal glass, with pillars of real gold, and glittering chandeliers in exquisite cut glass.

Terrace after terrace looks across views of exquisite beauty, and somehow one seems to breathe, as everywhere in the Russian capital, an atmosphere of enormous wealth and prosperity.

The morning that the Czar sent word he would visit the *Waturus* was one of vast excitement.

For hours beforehand, the entire wide river around us was cleared, and no vessels were allowed to pass up or down. The banks on either side were closed, no people or traffic was permitted, and guards and policemen were seen in all directions.

Around the yacht several boats containing policemen, guards and detectives patrolled up and down.

The flags were run up on the *Waturus*, crew and officers donned gala dress, the Archduke and Count Chorinsky wore admiral's uniform, and the ladies put on their most festive attire. All stood at attention on the upper deck, in places allotted to each.

The Empress came up the steps first, followed by the Czar, and his mother, the Empress Marie Feodorovna. They brought with them a large gathering of distinguished people, amongst whom were Queen Olga of Greece, the Crown Prince and Princess of Greece, with one of their sons, and the Grand Duchess Hélène of Russia.

The Empress was tall and stately, with exquisite colouring and beautiful fair hair; she seemed then most animated and gracious, and not at all as she had been until just before the present War.

In tremendous contrast appeared the Czar, so very short beside the Czarina, so painfully nervous and ill at ease, and his countenance of an ashen hue.

During the presentations he seemed scarcely able to speak with any degree of warmth and ease, and continually gazed about him from left to right in a painful nervous fashion. And this visit was strictly private and incognito. One felt a terrible pity for this monarch, who walked through life never knowing from hour to hour when his life would be taken. At any function or ceremony, the most extraordinary precautions have been taken, and there were nearly always six men dressed exactly like the Czar, for the sake of precaution.

Outside every room in the palace, guards have stood night and day, and have been changed suddenly at odd moments during the twenty-four hours.

Until even a short time before the present War, no one ever knew until a moment or two before luncheon or dinner was served in which room or hall these meals would be taken. You will hear, perhaps, this was one of the many peculiar customs of the Russian Court; in reality it was a matter of necessary precaution.

Not so very long ago, as the Royal Family were descending to lunch, the dining-hall was blown to pieces—luckily before any of the company reached it. In quite recent times, it happened, two or three moments before the Royal Family retired to rest, that every bed in the palace had mysteriously lost its coverings.

No one or nothing, until quite recently, has been very safe in the immediate entourage of the Russian Royalties; and it is no wonder that the once beautiful and most gracious Empress became a broken-down woman, and that day and night the little Czarevitch was never for one moment out of her sight.

The first difficult step that the Czarina had to encounter was the almost impossible task of trying to follow in the footsteps of her mother-in-law, a woman entirely her opposite, and from whom she received very little help or encouragement. The Empress Marie, from the time she was Princess Dagmar of Denmark, possessed a remarkable fascination and an inexhaustible energy in the pursuit of all pleasures, and at the same time was perfectly capable of coping with the many difficulties which have ever surrounded the Russian throne. She brought up the present Czar in such a manner that he was always under her influence, and never allowed any freedom; thus the early married years of the young Empress were beset with difficulties.

It is easy to imagine the terrible disappointment felt, and the very marked disapproval shown, at the birth of four daughters in succession; and, when at last an heir was born, so many tragic happenings had surrounded the throne that the nerves of the poor young Empress had become very much shattered, and she was obliged to retire more and more from Court functions and society generally.

There have been many stories current, in

and outside Russia, as to the mysterious accident which happened some few years ago to the Czarevitch, the effects of which he is said to bear to this day. From a high authoritative source one hears of that dreadful day through which the Czarina was forced to live on board the royal yacht, on which all the family were enjoying a peaceful cruise in far-away waters. One is told that those terrible fiends, the Nihilists, disguised as sailors, or attendants on the Imperial yacht, suddenly made some dastardly and inexplicable attack on the Czarevitch. So ghastly were the circumstances, that for the moment the Empress went mad and attempted to throw herself into the sea, and was only prevented at the very last moment by the timely interference of one of the lords-in-waiting. The whole terrible affair was hushed up, and many contradictory reports have spread far and wide.

To-day one hears that the health of the heir to the throne is almost completely restored. Let us hope that it is indeed the case, for the Russia of to-day, with its marvellous possibilities, is a changed land, and we are proud of this great country as our ally.

o

Does one realise what a sacrifice this great nation has made in forbidding the sale of vodka? Would any other European nation have been able to make such change? The effect upon the public life, generally, must be remarkable; and those who knew Russia before the War would be now astounded at the result of this enforced law.

Just before the War, when the Czar made a journey, troops lined the way; now Nicholas II takes a train journey like an ordinary man. The Czarina and her daughters wander freely forth, and minister to the sick and wounded garbed as nurses; and there is no danger for them in Russia to-day.

CHAPTER XVII

JOURNEYS ON THE " WATŪRŪS "

I T was early dawn one summer morning, and the sun was beginning to rise, when the *Watūrūs* left the great Russian capital. As we slowly sailed along the Neva, and looked back on the early morning sun flashing extraordinary lights on Petrograd, with its remarkable domed churches and turrets of gold, its magnificent river and sumptuous palaces on either side, we felt a distinct feeling of regret at leaving Russian soil.

One had approached this vast and powerful country with so many varied feelings, and uppermost a feeling of apprehension and insecurity, that one felt, perhaps, a deeper sense of regret in leaving its most generous and hospitable shores.

The return journey from Petrograd down the Baltic Sea proved, however, an immense delight to all, because Archduke Karl Stefan said he would take the yacht across to the coast of

195

Finland, so that we could cruise lazily in and out of the land of the Thousand Isles.

The Archduke engaged a special pilot, as the steering between those little islands—some of which are not more than seventy feet across —is most intricate and difficult.

The most beautiful part of the journey was reached between four and five o'clock in the morning, and of course we were all up on deck to watch the slow passage through these myriads of islets. The Northern atmosphere, which is so bewilderingly clear, with skies of most vivid colouring, helped to make the scene one of rare beauty. The sea was like a lake, and the little green islands, with their slender trees and wonderful shrubs, sent marvellous reflections into the intense blue of the waters.

We reached the capital, Helsingfors, about ten o'clock, and the Archduke insisted on our landing at once, and making a tour of this quaint Finnish town, which was an ideal little spot, with its buildings in red stone; and here and there other bright colours.

Later, the Archduke suggested our driving out into the country ; so a wait had to be made in the middle of the town, whilst Count

Chorinsky and Dr. Krumboldt went in search of five carriages.

There was great excitement among the inhabitants, whose curiosity was aroused by the strange-looking party of foreigners from the great white yacht in the harbour.

The drive was delightful, through remarkable scenery—some of which was of the wildest. We had tea, at the Archduke's suggestion, in the gardens of a little hotel ; and no one coming suddenly upon that gay and lively group could have believed it was that of the Imperial House of Austria.

Dinner, too, that night on the yacht was of the gayest ; and the scene, when we afterwards went up on deck, was too wonderful to describe. It was ten o'clock at least, and an extraordinary light shone over all, with the yacht at anchor in that quaint little harbour, with its twinkling lights, its music and laughter from the little town. At that hour, in that wondrous Northern light, it was quite possible even to read with comfort.

We left Helsingfors at four o'clock the next morning, and sailed away between more exquisite islands, rocks and little lakes to the fashionable little summer resort Hangoe, just a tiny collection of picturesque bath-houses and little villas.

Abo, the most exquisite little place I have ever seen, was reached at sunset. We glided into the little dream harbour under a flashing purple and rose sky, where everything was breathlessly still. Little boats, with yellow and red sails, shot out from unexpected corners, and drifted past the huge white floating palace of the Archduke.

Some of us went on land, but many preferred not to break the wonderful spell. It was enough to sit on deck, on that little dream lake, and watch the ever-changing lights, as a great ball of fiery red came up out of the lake, and cast a still more mystic light over all.

The superb scenery along the Finnish coast had a great effect on the Archduke. His enthusiasm and admiration for the ever-changing scene were tremendous. He certainly had a very artistic mind, and knew how to appreciate the beautiful, in the highest sense.

One day we sailed into Stockholm, famous for its harbour, which is supposed to be the most beautiful in the world. We remained there about a week. We had every opportunity of seeing the strange manners and customs of the people, especially out in the country parts, where the houses were exquisitely built in wood, and the dresses were so quaint and picturesque.

The King of Sweden was not in residence, so we received visits merely from the Ambassador and two Swedish Princesses.

Their Imperial Highnesses were asked if they desired to visit the palace with their party on board, but the Archduke, who now and again insisted on his sons and daughters doing things in a simple manner as ordinary folk, declined to visit the palace in a ceremonious fashion.

One afternoon he said we should all go and see the King's palace, as he particularly wanted to see some of the pictures in the famous gallery. One of the attendants ascertained that the public were admitted by card between the hours of two and four o'clock. Accordingly we were all rowed across, in several small boats, and walked to the King's palace, entering the building as ordinary visitors.

It appeared that parties of twenty at a time were conducted over the palace by a guide, who was somewhat aged, very slow and held forth at intervals on the works of art as we passed.

So we had to wait in the entrance until the party was complete. At first this greatly amused the Archduke, till we began slowly moving through the rooms, when the guide took too much time in enlarging upon some points, and only unlocked the rooms as he had finished.

This did not suit His Imperial Highness at all ; and he seemed to have quite forgotten that it was entirely his idea we were all seeing the King's palace under those circumstances.

Presently he became more and more impatient, striding up and down and talking in angry tones. Then he insisted on Count Chorinsky going to the guide, and telling him that he was Archduke Karl Stefan of Austria, who was in a great hurry, and that he must arrange for the rest of the party to wait until the Archduke and his party had inspected the entire palace.

There ensued much conversation. Count Chorinsky, in his usual diplomatic manner, tried to put the Archduke's message as courteously as possible, but the old guide remained obdurate. The only thing he would do, was to suggest that the Archduke and his party should return in a short time, and that then they could be conducted alone over the whole palace.

With much ingenious persuasion, that was what eventually happened. We all agreed it would have been more agreeable to have accepted the Ambassador's suggestion and visited the palace under his friendly guidance.

During my stay at the Austrian Court, I scarcely ever spoke German, and, as I have already said, my knowledge when I arrived was extremely limited. I must confess I passed through many unpleasant and awkward moments, and I was fully able to realise the drawbacks that many Englishwomen have been made to suffer by their limited knowledge of foreign languages.

Sometimes, in the very early morning, if we were passing any place of interest a bell would be rung, or one of the sailors would come to call us.

I think it was not long after we had left Stockholm that, one morning between four and five o'clock, I was awakened by the slowing down of the *Watürüs*, and the occasional ringing of a bell. Without drawing my curtains, I switched on the lights and hurriedly dressed, anxious to be on deck to see anything of interest that we might be near or passing.

Running along the corridor, and up the first flight of steps, I encountered one of the sailors in the dining-saloon, and knowing no Italian but sufficient German to ask, "What is it, please?" I was answered by a shake of the head and the word "Nebel."

Not remembering that as being the name of any place or town which we were supposed to pass that morning, I ventured to ask if there was anything to see.

The sailor very politely, but with a broad grin on his face, again shook his head, and said "Nichts"—one of the few words I really did know, meaning "nothing."

I therefore turned and retraced my steps, feeling very unhappy at having risen at such an early hour for nothing.

On returning to my cabin, I pulled back my curtains, still wondering why a stop should be made if there was nothing of importance to see.

Through the port-hole in the early morning light, I could distinguish nothing, and therefore settled down to read, to pass away the time. Meanwhile we seemed to move on again slowly, and from time to time I noticed that a bell still rang occasionally.

Presently we stopped dead again, and about six o'clock I sauntered up on deck to try and ascertain the reason of our early stay. A very thick fog entirely enveloped the yacht. Just then the same sailor came along the deck, and with a still broader grin said, in German, "There is still nothing to see."

That fog lasted all the morning; and, for the first time that I can ever remember, the Archduke looked quite anxious as he came down the steps of the bridge.

He said he would far rather face a great storm than the anxieties of a fog at sea.

Eventually we reached Karlskrona, where by that time our first real storm at sea overtook us. Thunder and lightning and a terrific gale came up; and, although at anchor, the *Watūrūs* was tossed about considerably.

After a very stormy night, we were able to

continue our journey next morning, and reached Copenhagen, that most enchanting Danish capital.

Many happy days were spent there, amidst the wonderful galleries, churches and museums, where so many of the statues by Thorvaldsen were to be seen.

Both the Marmor Church and Frue Church were beautiful, and in the latter, at the high altar, was that superb figure of " The Christ." On each side, down the entire length of the church, were still more remarkable figures, sculptured by the great man.

Our departure from Copenhagen was the occasion of much demonstration. In the harbour there were all kinds of shipping and several great warships, including an Austrian man-of-war.

The *Waturüs* was saluted on all sides as she passed out of harbour, sailors formed lines, and from the Austrian man-of-war the National Hymn and a popular military march burst forth from their splendid military band.

And once again we entered Kiel, our last stopping-place before disembarking—just a few last days to renew our acquaintance with that gay German watering-place, and then the great packing up commenced.

It was sad to leave the delightful yacht, all the young Archdukes and Archduchesses were loath to go. They loved those journeys on their father's yacht, where life for them became simple and informal, and the rigid etiquette and many rules were for awhile laid aside.

Directly we reached Kiel Station, one felt back again in the old world of ceremonies and un-realities.

State rooms were thrown open, the special train was there, and once again we steamed off to Zywiec Castle by way of Berlin, where a short but most interesting visit was made.

CHAPTER XVIII

THE ISLAND LUSSIN

TO arrive in Lussin on a January morning when one has left Vienna deep in snow, when one has rushed through days and nights filled with the pleasures of town life, dancing and skating, joyous hours at the Opera, and tasted the delights of the Vienna cafés! What an amazing change in a journey of twenty-four hours!

When the train, after plunging through the wilds of the Styrian and Julian Alps, at last skirts the mountainous shores of the Adriatic, lying soft and dazzlingly blue, and all the air is changed from a piercing cold to sunshine and warmth—then indeed can one truly say there is joy in contrasts.

At the busy but picturesque town of Trieste, one of the Archduke's beautiful yachts generally awaited us, so that the last eight or nine hours of the journey down the Adriatic to Lussin was made in luxurious comfort.

Sometimes we sailed direct to the island, at others, when the weather was particularly calm, and the wind in our favour, halts would be made at some of the ever-fascinating little isles, and the towns on the Istrian Coast.

Rovigno, a miniature Venice, full of antique remains and buildings, whose architecture at once called forth exclamations of surprise and enthusiasm, was always a favourite halt with the Archduke.

Next we reached the tiny isle of Brioni, with its rich Roman remains, its exquisite villas, little chapels built high up amidst great palm-trees, and scented Southern flowers, truly a spot of perfect beauty and peace. Very often we sailed across from Lussin, and explored the hidden wonders of this little island, and sometimes bathed in the clear warm waters which washed its shores.

Our next stoppage was almost a shock after the calm and peace of Brioni and Rovigno, for it was Pola, the important naval port of Austria, behind which rose the grey stone walls of the arena in whose arched enclosure once over fifteen thousand people witnessed the terrible struggles of gladiators and wild beasts, in the old Roman days.

The outer walls were in marvellous preservation, and the whole arena I found much larger and more magnificent than the more widely known one in Rome.

For many years Archduke Karl Stefan owned a beautiful villa in a delightful corner of Pola, where every year the Imperial Family spent some months, when the children were very young, and before the house on the island of Lussin was finished.

We generally reached Lussin when the long chain of Dinaric Alps on the mainland—which was distant about forty-five miles—began to put on its mysterious evening colours, and the sea reflected still more varied hues.

The island was divided into two parts; Lussin Piccolo, where was situated the little harbour, and the beautiful little piazza, with here and there a picturesque café, and a tiny hotel, with quaint and wonderful gardens, from which masses of colour showed up against dark cypress trees and shady palms; and Lussin Grande, with Monte Jovanni, on whose rugged and picturesque slopes was built the Archduke's white stone villa Podjavori.

Outside the enormous grounds, one or two

charming hotels and some beautiful villas were to be seen, besides a moderate-sized church and one or two very old and beautiful little chapels.

The inhabitants of Lussin are Italians, but every year in the season, from November to the beginning of April, wealthy Austrians from the capital and other towns, and indeed visitors of many nationalities flocked to this little isle on the Austrian Riviera, where summer was always smiling in that delicious, intoxicating Southern air, where life was all peace and simplicity, and where there were no bands or promenades, no roads for carriages or motors.

Podjavori itself was delightful, just a long, white, rambling stone building, two storeys high, furnished throughout in simple bungalow style, with corridors and stairs of grey marble. Its greatest charm was the glorious and superb views from its many casement windows, and flower-bedecked terraces, across the crystal blue waters of the Adriatic far down below, with its myriads of tiny isles, and the snow-clad Alps on the mainland beyond.

The garden was ideal, stretching far and wide on the wild and rugged slopes of Monte

P

Jovanni. It was full of surprises, with its steep and winding pathways and moss-grown steps, hewn out between great upstanding rocks, some of which were covered in marvellous growth, or else left projecting there, many feet high, just wild grey rocks towering up against an azure sky.

To the right and left one caught glimpses of gorgeous colouring from masses of rose-trees, groups of orange and lemon-trees, and scarlet camellias in between tall waving palms, and the low-spreading olive branches.

Dancing brown lizards jumped and skipped over the grey rocks; snakes glided and wriggled in the sun; and the warm and scented air, over this superb scene of beauty and peace, seemed to vibrate with the intoxicating murmur of myriads of insect life of the sunny South.

Ceremony was more or less waived during the stay of the Imperial Family on the island, and every one seemed to drop for a while the tedious restraint of Court life. Visitors came and went with far less formality, and the Archdukes and Archduchesses wandered about the tiny island, outside their own grounds, accompanied by one lady or gentleman of the Court.

Visitors to the island were quite accustomed to meet different members of the Imperial Family climbing up the steep paths of the mountain, or strolling on the little piazza. They were always very courteous and polite, and would stand and curtsy, or salute, whenever they met a Prince or Princess; but they never annoyed them by waiting about in groups and staring at them.

Tennis, boating, and expeditions to the countless small islands round formed the chief amusements of the day, but the young Archdukes and Archduchesses were always perfectly happy and content to wander, and explore the beauties of their extensive and rambling garden. They all were great gardeners. Each owned quite a large plot, and, although from time to time one of the many Italian gardeners—of whom there were about eighteen—gave them some assistance and advice, their private portions were the results mostly of their own labours.

Numerous birthdays and name-days occurred in those months spent in Lussin. If it was that of Her Imperial Highness, always the same order of ceremony was observed; one's smartest frock was donned; and the men wore full dress uniform.

After Mass, we assembled in the main entrance hall, the young Archduchesses and ladies carrying small nosegays, and all arrayed in the regulation white kid gloves; then we proceeded in procession to the boudoir of Her Imperial Highness, and offered our congratulations.

All the young Archdukes and Archduchesses went forward first and kissed their mother's hand, presented their floral offerings, and other gifts, nearly always of their own design and handiwork; then they each in turn recited some verses, each one in a different language.

Next the ladies and gentlemen of the suite advanced, made a very low bow, kissed the Archduchess's hand and murmured some appropriate words of felicitation.

The rest of the day was given over to festivities, a special dinner, and possibly an evening dance.

It nearly always happened that His Imperial Highness was away yachting on his birthday; then the young Princes and Princesses were obliged to write long letters, and each one had to be written in a different language. That was always considered rather an irksome task, but nevertheless some wonderful letters were written ; the Archduke always replied, but generally in English, a language which he wrote as correctly as he spoke.

The Princes and Princesses were also examined from time to time, with equal ceremony, even on the island.

Archduke Karl, whose day was nearly all study, went through many stiff examinations when his Imperial father and mother were present, his aide-de-camp in full parade dress and white gloves, and his various tutors and professors. One felt almost sorry for the young Prince at times, especially during the sojourn on the island, when from the early hour of six o'clock, and practically throughout the long sunny day, no relaxation was given to this eldest son of the Archduke.

Lussin, peopled by so many Italians, was famous for its religious ceremonies and processions.

Soon after my first arrival on the island, I was present at some of the solemn services which take place on Good Friday, and I was particularly impressed by the evening procession.

Good Friday, that year, fell early—at the beginning of April—and the weather in the South was just like our hottest August weather. Every one wore deepest mourning all day, and the Imperial Family attended all the services in the Parish Church on the island, instead of going to their little private chapel.

At ten o'clock in the morning we all proceeded in solemn procession, garbed in black, through the grounds of Podjavori, under a blazing sun, and the deepest of blue skies. Down across the dazzling white stone piazza by the side of the rocky shore, we went, to the Dome Church, which is, for the size of this tiny island, quite a large imposing church, very beautiful, very old and very Italian.

Special crimson and gold seats were set aside for the Imperial party at the altar rails; and the service lasted for about two hours, in the middle of which a lengthy sermon was delivered by Don Antonio, the old Italian priest of Lussin.

Again at three o'clock, we proceeded in the same order to the church, and an early dinner took place at six o'clock to enable us to be present at the evening service. I might mention that on Wednesdays and Fridays in Lent no

meat was ever allowed at any of the meals, and
on the last four days in Lent neither meat, nor
eggs, nor butter, nor milk was allowed. To vary
the menu on these days, the *chef* must have
required remarkable skill and thought, for it
seemed that the most wonderful dishes appeared,
notwithstanding, during all these times.

The first Good Friday evening stands out
very vividly in my mind, for on entering the
church, which I have explained was truly
immense, we found it lit with nothing but
candles, and packed to overflowing with a
seething mass of picturesque Italians. Around
the top of the walls of this very lofty church
was a tiny gallery ; and along this, round
the entire church, were hundreds of lighted
candles.

By some mistake, on entering the church—
which was certainly most bewildering and very
weird—one of the ladies and myself found
ourselves separated from the Imperial party,
and not wishing to make a fuss we slipped quietly
into a seat on the right-hand side of the church,
four or five rows from the top.

At the beginning of the service, every one
was presented with an enormous candle quite

three feet high. The next proceedings were very sudden, and almost grotesque, because I found, to my dismay, that we had seated ourselves on the wrong side of the church, apparently, for on the right-hand side, where we sat, there were only men. A bell rang suddenly, and all the men around us—there seemed many hundreds—stood up and began to put on long white flowing habits, with white hoods and girdles. The scene was amazing, and it was a very long time before we could succeed in pushing our way through this struggling mass of humanity, in that dim religious light.

We did eventually, breathless and bewildered, each clutching our enormous candle, push our way out, and stood at the bottom of the aisle to await the next event.

Then all the clergy came down from the high altar, with Don Antonio in magnificent purple vestments carrying the Cross under a great embroidered canopy.

They paused opposite to the Imperial Family, who followed on down the aisle in procession with the ladies and gentlemen of the suite. Then came the servants of the household, the nuns from the cloisters of Lussin, and the general congregation, numbering many hundreds, all with their candles lighted, and the men wearing those extraordinary white garments.

Down the many steps of the church, and on down to the piazza went this long procession, walking in twos. The moon by this time was shining full and bright ; all the visitors of Lussin had flocked to see this wonderful sight, and were grouped on either side of the way, as we proceeded to walk through the principal parts of the island.

In the windows of every villa, every tiny house and hut on the hill and mountain-side, two lighted candles were placed, and the singing of this vast crowd was superb. We walked on and on, and actually entered and passed through two other churches, and wended our way up and down and round, until at last we returned to the big Dome Church, after walking for at least two hours.

The scene was indescribably weird and solemn ; the heavenly night with its purple sky, and the lights dancing on the water, and the slowly moving procession going ever onwards, with its lighted candles, was a sight which one can truly say is seldom seen. In fact, only in Lussin and in Pola, I understand, does this particular procession, in this peculiar manner, take place.

CHAPTER XIX

FESTIVITIES ON THE ISLAND

EASTER was very often spent by the Imperial Family in Lussin, and it came as a welcome and joyous relaxation after the monotony of Lent, and the solemnities of Good Friday in which we had all just partaken.

Easter Sunday was given over to great rejoicings, rules were put on one side, and the Princes and Princesses were practically free to do what they pleased. There was always a very elaborate lunch, to which Don Antonio and other priests were invited, besides any chance friends of Their Imperial Highnesses who were staying at their villas, or at the hotels on the island.

Then followed always the egg hunt, in the grounds of Podjavori, an Easter custom which is still observed in several other European countries. Beautiful and enormous eggs, containing costly gifts, and the choicest bonbons, to each of which a name was attached, were hidden in that portion of the extensive grounds given over to the hunt.

Every one donned gala attire ; the day was usually perfect weather, and the scene was always one of gaiety and amusement for young and old.

Another custom, which struck one as being very quaint, was the placing in every one's apartment of a plate containing a dozen hard-boiled eggs, painted over in various bright colours, and another plate on which was found various kinds of cold meat. As it was obvious no one ever felt the need of this strange food, these curious gifts were immediately sent down to be given to the poor.

On Easter Monday Lussin's little regatta took place, which was looked upon by all as if it were as great an event as the races at Kiel, or as important as the Cowes Regatta.

It proved that both Their Imperial Highnesses and visitors alike were content to lead the simple life on that little Adriatic isle, and from it they derived many days of wonderful gaiety and much amusement.

Their Imperial Highnesses always gave their patronage ; and, if they were not able to be present themselves, Admiral Count Chorinsky was sent.

During all the years I spent at the Austrian Court, I received many delightful invitations, much favour and many kindnesses in Vienna and especially in Lussin, where every season the same gathering of distinguished visitors, and military and naval officers, were to be met.

I had much free time, and the very kind permission of Their Imperial Highnesses to attend the many tennis and sailing parties, dances and dinners, and bridge parties, to which I was frequently invited.

It was indeed a gay world, filled with days of delight, amidst scenes of glory and magnificence which can only be found in the unfrequented tracks on the Adriatic shores.

In no country can one find just the same happy-go-lucky, charming people as the hospitable and light-hearted Austrians.

Chaperoned and introduced by Madame Karger, wife of General Karger, Baroness Thiesbaert, or Countess Huyn, I soon became acquainted with every one worth knowing in Lussin.

Night after night dances were given; there was no fuss of driving to and fro, one just walked through the beautiful grounds in the soft, scented night air. I always had plenty of escort, as all the men attached to the suite of the Archduke's household were most courteous and affable, and were of course invited to all that took place in Lussin.

They were all great dancers and sportsmen, especially the naval commander of the yacht, Captain Cohanyi, a delightful and very handsome Hungarian, and Herr Theodorovitch, a gay and very frivolous Pole.

Captain Lyst, too, was always at the dances, and Count Chorinsky, the man who, during all my stay at the Imperial Court, proved a real friend, a most amusing travelling companion, and succeeded in helping me through many of the intricacies and difficulties one met with in such a strange world.

Holding a somewhat independent position, with a great deal of freedom attached, it was natural that I should be subjected to a fair share of petty annoyances, jealous remarks

and insinuations from the various people to
be met at a foreign court. But on looking back
on any unpleasantness, somewhere in the
background, by his extraordinary tact, Count
Chorinsky was sure to be able to put in a
timely word which always had a miraculous
result.

When the high spirits of the young Archdukes
—often far beyond the control of their respective
tutors or attendants—reached some disastrous
point, if the Count happened to be anywhere
near, somehow it always appeared easier to
settle matters peacefully. One day, one of the
young Princesses, only a year or so before she
was grown up, lay in wait behind some tall
bushes and rocks in the gardens at Lussin,
with a large water hose ready to turn on to
some unfortunate maid who had, perhaps,
incurred her displeasure. I happened to be
coming up one of the winding orange groves,
and came unexpectedly into the full play of
the hose raised ready for action. In a second I
was drenched to the skin, and felt and looked a
sorry spectacle.

Shrieks of delight were raised by the Princess
at the mistake she had made, which were

suddenly hushed by the voice of the Count, who had come to the window of his study, overlooking one of the terraces. Quickly engaging the Princess in some trivial conversation by asking her if she would be kind enough to turn the hose on to some of the special flowers on his balcony, he dropped unobtrusively on my path, as I was trying to make good an undignified escape, one of his long military cloaks.

The incident—but a trivial one—might have proved much more unpleasant. In a few minutes, to escape unnoticed would have been impossible. People from all directions would have appeared, endless questions would have been put : Why was the Princess unattended ? Who left the hose in that particular spot, and so on.

The next evening, it happened, I was returning from a ball at one of the hotels in the early hours of the morning. I had been brought to the lodge gates of the park by my chaperon ; as there was no means of driving on the island, and no one outside the Court was allowed in the grounds, one had to walk a good ten minutes through those superb, though lonely, grounds to reach the house. But no one ever minded that. The nights in the South seemed always the best time of the day, with the delicious cool air, heavy with the scent of orange blossom, roses and lilies, and when the moonlight shone over the distant snow-tipped mountains, showing up Lussin and the tiny islands around under strangely beautiful evening lights.

Generally there would have been several of us returning to the house, but it happened that my only escort through the park at that unfortunate hour in the morning was the extremely handsome and very gay Pole, one of Archduke Karl's attendants. We had always been great friends, and were often at the same parties, yachting expeditions, dances, and tennis parties.

Podjavori was the only residence of the Imperial Family that was more or less kept up without ceremony. The various entrances and doors were left entirely unguarded during the daytime, and left open without the regulation official standing just inside; and at night they were simply locked. If one wished to return late at night, it was quite possible to ask for

Q

one of the keys of the doors from the major-domo, and I generally entered by a little side door from one of the terraces nearest to my own apartments.

By some most unfortunate mishap, on nearing the door, I found to my distress I had lost my key; in fact, after thinking for a few seconds, I distinctly remembered having left it on my dressing-table.

It was certainly a most unenviable position to be stranded outside a royal residence, between three and four o'clock in the morning, alone with one of the male members of the Archducal suite, whose own apartments were in a separate building, and who seemed to have no practical suggestions to offer, but was inclined to look upon the whole thing as a tremendous joke.

There was no means of making anyone hear; there was only one bell, which was at the main entrance of the château, and if rung it would certainly be heard by some of the Imperial Family. No, there was no way out. I should have to return to the hotel, knock up the night porter, and try and secure an entrance somehow, knowing full well the story—or rather, quite another story—would be all over the island in the morning, and in all probability I should be asked to resign my connection with the Imperial Family.

In vain I implored my Polish friend to return to his quarters and to leave me to try and right matters alone, but he protested it was impossible to leave me to wander through the grounds alone, and along the piazza leading to the hotel. There were no lamps or lights on the island, and even under the light of a moon, some of the rugged paths and avenues of cypress trees were very dark and difficult to follow.

At last we set off in gloomy silence, for even the ever-bubbling spirits of the Pole began to diminish as he began to realise the awkward position. We had only gone a few steps down a steep incline of the grounds, when we heard footsteps approaching, and saw two men coming up the pathway. Thinking, I suppose, to shield me, my companion caught hold of my arm and drew me behind some projecting rocks, saying it was perhaps wiser to let the on-comers pass without seeing us. But, alas, it was too late ! As the figures of the two men reached our temporary hiding-place, the well-known voice of the chaplain called out :

"Whoever is in hiding, I am afraid you were seen."

"Yes, better come out," added Count Chorinsky, in his drawling, mocking voice.

The Count never betrayed surprise at anything, but on that occasion—for perhaps a second—a look of blank astonishment crossed his face when he saw who we were. Before I could even begin to explain, he turned in a laughing, cool way to the rather shocked chaplain, who was not a favourite with many, and said :

"Another practical joke, I suppose, of the English Miss. Too bad to lie in wait and scare us like this. I asked her to wait for my escort to-night, and I am afraid we have kept her waiting. Let's all get on to the house. Good night," he said curtly to the Pole with a nod of dismissal.

We went up to the house, the Count talking hard all the time. At the chaplain's door we paused a moment to wish him good night, and the Count said :

"Come along, Miss Nellie. I'll give you

those letters and see you to your door. You mustn't give me away," he called back to the chaplain, " for keeping the Miss waiting about so long. Good night. Now," he said, as he strode along, " what on earth made you do such a risky thing ? "

I was almost in tears by this time as I burst out :

" I have lost my key and I was going back to the hotel."

" *Gott im Himmel*," he exclaimed, " that's bad," and he stood still and looked at me. " I don't know how I am going to help you. Of course you could come to my villa," he said, smiling. " My man wouldn't say a word—but you'd still have to get back in the morning." Then he frowned, and said, " How could you be so——Look here, there is just a remote chance that my man may have the keys of some of the doors which he had to use in going in and out to attend on Count —— when he was staying in that part of the house."

In less than five minutes he was back with his valet, who always sat up for him, and in his hands he held some keys, one of which opened the door.

The story was never told, but it might have been—and in a very different manner—if I had happened to run into anyone else but the chivalrous, and ever-trustworthy Count Chorinsky.

CHAPTER XX

CRUISES IN THE ADRIATIC

MANY royal and distinguished visitors came to Lussin. During the long, tedious waits and presentations attending their arrival, when we all stood about in groups—often feeling bored and weary—Count Chorinsky would be sure to introduce the various members of the suite to one another; and a tiring half-hour would quickly pass, helped on by his subdued chatter, and his ever-ready witty remarks.

Archduchess Marie Josepha used to pay a flying visit, sometimes of two days, on her yacht. One could not help admiring her tremendously. She was so gracious, so tall and elegant, and one felt her life had indeed been a tragedy. One of her ladies-in-waiting was Countess Attems. She was, perhaps, one of the smartest and best-dressed Viennese

231

women whom I ever met. She was extraordinarily gay and witty, and was always
particularly kind to me. She was a great
friend of Their Imperial Highnesses, and would
come and stay by herself for several days,
when she was off duty from Archduchess Marie
Josepha. Once or twice she was a guest on the
yacht for some days at a time, and her presence
added greatly to the gaiety and amusement of all.

The late Franz Ferdinand and his morganatic
wife also visited the island, and proved themselves very amiable and kindly disposed to all
those who were presented to them.

Prince and Princess August of Saxe-Coburg,
the Duchess of Würtemberg, Archduke Leopold
—all near relatives of Their Imperial Highnesses—were also frequent visitors, and seemed
to love the peace and quiet of the little fairy
isle, where for a while they could shake off all
Court ceremonies and indulge in that rare sense
of absolute freedom.

Venice, being so near, was often visited. I
remember one March being informed that I
should be required to accompany Their Imperial
Highnesses the next day for a fortnight's stay
in that romantic Italian city.

That was the most informal cruise I took with the Archduke and Archduchess; no lords or ladies-in-waiting were in attendance, and only Archduchess Mechtildis and her two brothers, one governess and maids were taken.

We left Lussin early in the morning, and the *Waturus* glided out of the harbour before many of the inhabitants were aware of its departure. We called at Pola for Prince and Princess August of Saxe-Coburg—the latter was Archduchess Maria Theresa's sister—and they both accompanied Their Imperial Highnesses to Venice, and remained with them for the two weeks' sojourn.

Venice, at all times, and under any circumstances, is ever a most fascinating and wonderful city, but to see it for the first time from the decks of a royal yacht is a delight experienced by very few.

We anchored in the Grand Canal, almost opposite the Doge's Palace, the Grand Piazza, and in sight of the Church Marie de Salute. We remained there about two weeks in that glorious position, where by day and by night, with the ever-changing skies, and by the light of a full moon, Venice could be seen at its very best.

Whenever Archduke Karl Stefan went to Venice, he always hired the same two gondolas, which were attached to the side of the yacht, so that we had the joy of being taken about by the same gondoliers, who in this case knew only too well who were their distinguished patrons, and took particular care.

For the first day or two, we were anchored between the yacht of the notorious Archduke Otto and that of Count Malewski, a very wealthy Russian, and one of the Archduke's great friends.

As usual, there were many distinguished guests who visited the *Watürüs*, the first being Archduke Otto, the first cousin of Archduchess Maria Theresa, who remained to luncheon with his aide-de-camp.

When I was presented to this gay, and much-discussed Archduke, and I heard his amusing and entertaining conversation at lunch, it seemed impossible to believe the horrid tales one heard of certainly one of the handsomest men at Court. Champagne-drinking is said to have brought about his ruin ; in later years he consumed untold quantities, and was very seldom sober. No one seems to have had the least control over him ; but, although his numerous escapades and his many practical jokes caused untold scandal to his regiment, he was extremely popular with the men.

He seems to have commenced very young, for at an early date we hear of his insulting his colonel at a mess dinner because he had severely reprimanded him the previous day. He suddenly seized the drum, which he had previously caused to be filled with champagne, and leaping on to the table smashed it on the colonel's head. It may be said that he was not responsible for such an act, but in Vienna the name of Archduke Otto is never very flatteringly spoken of. There are very few restaurants or cafés in which he did not commit some wild or unfortunate escapade, and one must feel much sympathy for Archduchess Marie Josepha, who besides all the untold horrors she was forced to see, has had the great responsibility of guarding, educating, and entirely bringing up the present heir to the throne, Archduke Karl Franz Josef.

The Austrian nation has felt a deep relief, a great thankfulness, that not the slightest trace of Archduke Otto's many unpleasant, and unspeakably bad traits, has ever been found in the charming and very popular young Archduke. His bringing up has been extraordinarily difficult, but in his early youth he was kept away from every possible evil contact. He spent some time at a big English-speaking school, which must have been an unusually good training for an Austrian Archduke.

Only the other day I was speaking with some one who had been with him a great deal before the war, and who spoke in terms of the greatest admiration and enthusiasm of the young heir, adding that he was every inch a man, a great sportsman, and possessed a strong personality.

Many people have feared that in recent years the deeply religious atmosphere of his mother's house may have had a wrong influence over him, but this does not seem to have been the case. Then, too, his marriage to Princess Zita has so far proved a happy and successful one.

Princess Zita possesses a quiet intelligence, and has, I believe, been partly educated in England. She comes from a beautiful home, where, in spite of the difficulty of bringing up twenty-one children, everything has been done

with an admirable method, almost impossible
to imagine.

Some time ago I received a letter from a lady,
attached for many years to the suite of the Duke
of Parma. She described what a merry, delightful household it was at that time. She said
that even then there were twenty children at
home, one Prince only having left to marry a
daughter of Archduke Friedrich. They never
sat down to table less than twenty-five or
thirty persons. Everything was arranged on a
gigantic scale, of course; riding and driving
parties were always a big procession and
attracted the greatest attention. The castle
at Schwarzau am Steinfelde, where they spent
half the year, was a magnificent place, but they
all loved better their Italian home, Pianore bei
Viareggio, some distance from Florence, where
many delightful months were spent every year.

I received a letter after the wedding of
Princess Zita to the present Austrian heir,
describing the elaborate ceremony, and telling
me of the genuine liking they all felt for the
young Archduke. Especially with the Hungarians was he much more beloved, because
from early boyhood he had acquired a complete

mastery of their language. Most surely he is much more popular with the majority of Austrians than the late Archduke Franz Ferdinand, whose bigoted tendencies and almost superstitious nature failed to gain any good influence over certain sets of people, and who was perhaps a little jealous of the nephew who was one day to take the throne of Austria, which he secretly coveted for his own son.

I heard a little story not so very long ago from some one who was present at a dinner given by the late Archduke Franz Ferdinand. One of the guests was the present heir to the throne, then a young man of about nineteen years. The principal table decoration, placed immediately in front of the young Archduke, was an enormous and elaborate ice centre-piece, with the crown of Austria most exactly reproduced in ice. When the dinner was well advanced and every one had become warmed up with the wines and toasts of the evening, Archduke Franz Ferdinand so contrived that some one should seem to urge the young Archduke to lift the crown of ice and place it on his own head. This the present heir did. Lifting it slowly from its resting place, he placed the fast-melting ice crown on his head, which, with the excitement and heat of the rooms, was almost at fever heat. Incoherently he seems to have spoken the words : " I crown myself Emperor of Austria and King of Hungary." Toasts were again drunk, speeches made, but the crown of ice was fast melting on the head of Austria's future heir. Archduke Franz Ferdinand was evidently not prepared for his own untimely end. Let us hope that the ill omen of the ice crown will not alight upon Austria's present heir, who, from all one hears, is better able to bear the crown than many other members of the Court of Austria.

But to return to Venice, where, for the first time, I was presented to the father of the present heir to the throne, and where we often saw him sitting at the little tables on the piazza of St. Mark's, or mingling with the fashionable promenaders.

All the days we spent there were amusing and delightful. Mornings were passed gliding round the canals, either with the Archduke, or the Archduchess, and Prince and Princess August of Saxe-Coburg, often stopping to visit the beautiful churches and the many famous

galleries. Sometimes some of us would go off
with the Archduke to find some remote and
artistic view of Venice that he had perchance
not yet attempted to paint.

At night we would be serenaded by masked
singers in brilliantly illuminated gondolas, who
would glide along the canal towards the *Watürüs*
and sing some of those haunting and wondrously
beautiful Italian songs. Sometimes we left
the *Watürüs*, and took our own gondolas in
the evening, and moved with the rest of the
gay procession that wended its way nightly
down the grand canal, and paused awhile before
the brightly lighted palaces and hotels, from
which again music would be poured forth into
our willing ears.

There were many voyages taken on the
Watürüs before it was put on one side, and
another took its place. When the Emperor
sent Karl Stefan as his representative to the
coronation of the King of Spain, the *Watürüs*
was used. Naples, and the northern coast of
Africa were also visited, and the many, many
delightful places on both sides of the Adriatic
were continually being visited and explored.

Towards the end of May one year, the Archduke proposed to journey down the entire length of the Adriatic as far as Athens, so that a thorough acquaintance of its many charms and beauties could be made, and a comparison between the Dalmatian coast and the Italian side could be enjoyed.

We left Lussin in the morning, with the usual ceremonious leave-taking, which in Lussin was always touched with a genuine sorrow at the departure of Their Imperial Highnesses. Pretty Italian children lined the way from the gates of Podjavori, with masses of beautiful flowers, and dropped the petals of many roses along the road; all the visitors assembled in the little harbour, and the Burgomaster and Don Antonio were ready with speeches and charming words of farewell.

As we sailed out of Lussin, and looked back on its wild and rocky heights, with the gaily dressed Italians still waving from various points on the island, to which they had scrambled in their eagerness to catch the last glimpse of the yacht, and the groups of visitors who still stood about on the little white piazza, we were struck anew with the beauty and charm of this particular Adriatic isle.

R

Sebenico and Spalato we sailed past without stopping, and then we cruised between many little rocky islands, till we dropped anchor at the grey stone island of Lissa, with its rugged heights and the little isles around. At once the boats of the *Waturus* were lowered, so that we might all be rowed across to the famous caves on the little island of Bussi, the most marvellous being the famous Blue Grotto, which is so often compared with the better known one of Capri, as to the beauty of which opinions very often differ.

Our visit to these historic caves was marked by an amusing but somewhat risky adventure.

The Archduke and Archduchess left in the first boat, and the second boat was occupied by two of the Princesses and some of the suite. I followed in the next boat with Mademoiselle, Herr Theodorovitch, one of the Princesses, four or five sailors, rowing, and Captain Cohanyi in command; maids and servants followed in the next.

There was a heavy swell, and it was quite difficult to get along. But, besides that, water began oozing in at the bottom and sides of our boat, and gradually in a rather more rapid manner.

The Captain kept an immovable countenance, but gave orders to three of the sailors to bale out, whilst the other two rowed on as quickly as possible. When the water became so evident that it was necessary to put our feet up on the seats, and to hold tightly our wet skirts, the officer at last thought it advisable to call out to the boat in front to keep close, as he thought our boat was leaking with rather alarming rapidity. The Archduke, having caught the sounds of shouting, and noticing the looks on our faces, called out to know what was happening.

He was not in the least perturbed, but seemed to enjoy our plight. He stood up in his boat, and laughingly shouted across to us not to mind, that there were two boats close at hand ready to take us on board.

It was an alarming few minutes, and we were all relieved to enter the shelter of the caves, even though landing was not possible. The waters were calm, and the walls of the cave could easily be reached.

But there was no hole in the boat and no

leakage, and the water of its own accord gradually stopped making its way into the boat.

The mystery was afterwards explained. It appeared that that particular boat had not been used, or let into the water during the hot weather at all; and hanging up always in the terrific heat of the sun, this had caused the planks of wood to shrink considerably, so that the cracks of the boat had become very wide indeed. Hence the sudden inrush of the waters, until the wood had become sufficiently enlarged to fill up the cracks.

As soon as we had recovered from the scare, we awoke to the fact that we were slowly passing through cave after cave, where the water was an ever-changing colour, from the deepest turquoise to the faintest possible blue, with stones and bits of rock at the bottom shining and gleaming like jewels. The light was the same weird, fantastic blue, rugged glittering walls were around us, and the boats glided one after the other, very slowly and carefully. The light reflected on us bathed all in wondrously beautiful colours, so that in glancing back, as we went through each narrow passage and cavern, one could easily imagine it was a scene from fairyland.

Once more on board, notwithstanding our wet clothes and feet, and the thought that in another two or three minutes—as the officer afterwards informed us—we should have all been in the sea, we agreed that the Blue Grotto was one of the most remarkable bits of nature that any of us had ever seen.

After that, the Archduke gave orders to steam right across the Adriatic to the Italian coast, down which we went, until the little town of Barletta was reached. We landed at once, and made a short and quick tour of this quaint Italian town, followed, as we were in all our Italian visits, by quite a crowd, and with detectives on bicycles. The Italian officials were extremely particular at the moment of our landing, all passports were minutely scrutinised and many questions asked.

The next little halt we made was at the picturesque town of Trani, with its delightful Italian villas and gardens, where quantities of Southern flowers and plants abounded.

A hurried visit was paid to St. Nicholas, a very old and wonderful church, where the carvings and statues were exquisite. The crypt, which ran under the entire church, was fitted up as a beautiful chapel ; and here we heard Mass in the morning.

At Bari, after having exhausted the sights of the little town, the Archduke suggested a long drive out into the beautiful Italian country, where we passed along avenues of blooming mimosa and masses of roses and palm-trees.

Before we went on board, and we had made exhaustive purchases in the town, the Archduke insisted on buying a little black goat, which very much took his fancy. Needless to say, the difficulty of getting the animal on board was immense, besides the business of duty to be paid, and all the fuss which arises when one takes anything away from a foreign country. We stayed at anchor a day or so at Bari, so that the little goat was able to find its bearings.

CHAPTER XXI

LAST GLIMPSES OF THE ADRIATIC

THE journey down to Brindisi was made through a heavy and rolling sea, when nearly every one on board was ill, and we were not more than two or three to sit at table.

Then, indeed, the *Waturus* presented a sorry sight. Archduke Karl Stefan insisted that it was far better for every one who was ill to lie on cushions and mattresses on the upper deck than to remain in the cabins.

Archduke Karl Stefan never suffered from sickness, but used to stride about the decks, making endless suggestions and inquiries ; and, if one were not ill, almost compelling one to say at what precise moment one imagined the catastrophe would occur.

I always felt so sorry for every one, although I must confess a rough sea was a source of infinite joy to me.

A stay of two or three days was made in that busy harbour where the great P. & O. vessels were to be seen. The town itself we did not find beautiful ; but the country around, with its vineyards and quantities of immense cactus trees, was exceedingly beautiful.

We left Brindisi at night, and were all up by five o'clock the next morning to enjoy the magnificent journey into Corfu, that most enchanting of Grecian islands, rising to a great height, and affording such superb views of mountainous country. We spent many days there, and were again charmed with the grandeur of the scenery, and the surpassing beauty of the Achilleion.

Patras, so exquisite from the sea, was disappointing on land. So we hurried away and made straight for Athens, passing down the famous canal of Corinth, and anchoring at Phallerius, the harbour of Athens, where ships from every country in the world seemed to have gathered.

Many visits of ceremony were made in this famous Grecian capital, to the late King of Greece, to the Crown Prince and Princess, and to many others.

It was on this particular cruise that the Archduke was seized with one of his· many curious ideas.

One day the order went round that His Imperial Highness wished it to be understood that none but those of the Imperial Family were to leave or return to the yacht other than by using the rope ladders. The staircases which every one had been accustomed to use were, for the future, to be for the sole benefit of the Imperial Family. There was great consternation, and every one expressed much indignation. Poor Countess Huyn and the other ladies, and even the maids were all equally perturbed. It certainly was a surprising command from the Archduke. For some time, unless one was obliged, no one left the yacht, or contrived to do so when His Imperial Highness was on land ; then the commanding officer, in ordering the boats to be swung out, conveniently forgot this order, and the sailors stood ready at the usual staircase.

But there were some amusing incidents ; the Archduke took to standing and watching the departures, and kept a strict look-out for the returns. It was no joke for anyone at all nervous, even when the vessel was at anchor, to ascend and descend a rope ladder, especially when the yacht was perhaps very high out of the water, and the tide was low. One felt so very sorry for some of the ladies who were not very agile, or accustomed to gymnastics.

Fortunately the Archduchess intervened, and managed to suggest it might be rather a dangerous proceeding if a storm came up, or a heavy swell from a passing steamer overtook the yacht.

When the Grecian Royal Family visited the *Watūrǔs*, great preparations were made ; and masses of immense pink carnations were handed to me to arrange on the tea-tables. I had long since taken over, on the yacht, the duty of arranging the numerous magnificent flowers that were so often sent on board.

The Grecian Royal Family were charming, the old King especially—who was Queen Alexandra's favourite brother—being so gracious and kind. When my turn came to be presented, he chatted a long time in most excellent English ; and he made a point of saying some charming word to every one. The rest of the party, including the Crown Prince and Princess, were equally gracious, and expressed delight with all they saw. The Crown Princess was the sister of the German Emperor.

The many delights of this most famous historical capital were greatly appreciated; and we spent a whole day amongst the great ruins on that rocky summit called the Acropolis.

We were taken through all the wonderful remains, the temples and old churches, by an excellent guide, who explained very carefully all the great history connected with this most interesting mass of ruins.

One day the Archduke gave a big lunch at the Hôtel Bretagne in Athens, where a most enjoyable time was spent, and where the menu was quite a mixture of Grecian, Italian and French dishes.

The journey through the Ionian Islands, passing Cephalonia—with its chief town Agostolle, where we halted for some time—Itaka, Santa Maura and Zante, was just as extraordinarily impressive as that other journey through the Northern isles on the Finnish coast. In this case, the weird Southern light, on the gigantic mountains around, cast extraordinary reflections into the sea; and the whole beauty of these numerous Grecian isles was, perhaps, on a grander scale.

Another short stay was made at Corfu, which we were all enchanted to revisit ; after which we began the tour of the much-talked-of Dalmatian coast.

In my estimation the town of Ragusa, which I heard dated back many hundreds of years, and was built by the Greeks, was the most beautiful place on the whole of this coast.

The yacht was anchored at Gravosa, its port, which was possibly two miles away. Then we drove up and up, far above the blue Adriatic, which was dashing against the wild and rugged rocks, along a wonderful roadway, with here and there a flaming garden, and wonderful old walls and doorways, overhung with masses of flowering plants, orange branches and every kind of Southern growth.

The entrance to this ancient town was grandly beautiful, and through the old gateway, Porta Pille, one reached the little narrow high street called the Corso, every building in which dated centuries back and contained marvellous relics of the past.

One fell under the spell of Ragusa immediately,

GRAVOSA, THE PORT OF RAGUSA, DALMATIA

and it was not difficult to imagine the many vicissitudes through which the old town had passed ; indeed, one ran up against the signs of its struggles and its triumphs at every corner.

We spoke with the brown-robed Franciscan monks, in their fine old cloister, and learnt of the tales of siege, of the plague which carried off thousands of citizens ; we were pointed out the gigantic fortifications which were then built, and told of the years of prosperity and peace which followed, till those terrible earth-quakes shook the very foundations and wrought such untold havoc.

For the Austrian Empire Ragusa has fought many fierce battles, in which thousands of men from the gallant little town have perished ; and one was struck at the wonders that still remain, in spite of the storms and stress of centuries.

Archduke Karl Stefan was kindness itself in pointing out its many beautiful features ; he seemed to know every corner.

We lingered long in Piazza dell' Erbe, the principal square ; and, as it happened to be market-day, it was filled with a medley of gorgeous costumes. There were Montenegrins, with their white coats, embroidered waistcoats, and red and black caps ; picturesque peasants from Bosnia and Herzegovina ; gipsies from Serbia ; and here and there men in full Turkish costume, their little jackets embroidered with exquisite colouring and design.

Archduchess Maria Theresa made extensive purchases, ordering several of the most charming and elaborate costumes, which could be worn at the various fancy dress carnivals, in which the young Archdukes and Archduchesses always took such delight.

I remember at the time, when the massive fortifications and gigantic walls were pointed out to us, being so impressed with the apparent strength of the town, with its superbly elevated position. Then all was peace and security, particularly in this little ancient city, which conveyed the impression that it was resting contentedly after its years of strife in the years gone by.

And within a few years of that day the world is at war. The Austrians are fighting the Italians, and Ragusa is one of the towns that has suffered considerably.

On that gorgeous May morning, when last I visited Ragusa, in the little shops—which were

made to open wide and looked quite oriental,
particularly in the Corso—Dalmatians sat
cross-legged in their picturesque garb, peacefully
making extravagantly beautiful embroideries
and fascinating garments, which one saw were
similar to those worn by the people around.

How difficult it was to tear ourselves away
from that enchanting town, but, as the Archduke
pointed out, there was so much more to be seen.

And the beautiful white yacht sailed away,
only a short distance over the deep blue waters
to the little island of La Croma. How grandly
majestic the antique walls, the old houses with
their scarlet roofs showed up above the Adriatic,
which was there so clear that one could distinguish the gliding forms of the fish, and the
curious stones and rocks below.

An ancient monastery, belonging to white-
robed Dominican monks, and set in a luxuriant
background of roses and a wealth of flaming
flowers, gave us hospitable welcome ; but the
stay was brief, as we were due at Spalato at a
certain time.

The Imperial Family had often visited and
explored that particular town, so there were
only two or three on board who did not already

know its charms. The Archduke most kindly telegraphed, from Ragusa to Spalato, for the famous Dr. Bulic, that learned director of the great museum, and the historian of Spalato, to meet the yacht on its arrival, so as to be ready to accompany a small party round his ancient town.

This struck me as being extraordinarily thoughtful and generous. The party consisted of only another lady besides myself and one of the gentlemen of the suite, and for three people Archduke Karl Stefan was perfectly willing to drop anchor, and permit us a delightful day on land, whilst the whole Imperial Family remained on board. Thoughtfulness for others is not a characteristic generally attributed to the much-abused Hapsburgs ; but, in the case of Archduke Karl Stefan and Archduchess Maria Theresa, at least, it is especially noticeable.

As we sailed into Spalato, our attention was immediately arrested by the magnificent array of buildings which were the remains of the famous Palace of Diocletian.

So immense was this palace, which took twelve years to build, that the town of Spalato had actually been built within its ancient walls.

Dr. Bulic was on the quay, waiting with a carriage ; and we spent a most interesting and instructive day with him.

The marvels pointed out to us were indeed worth seeing : the streets with their ancient columns and great archways, the market-place, with its crowds of men and women from the East, in every conceivable costume, trying to sell their wares, some of which had come in by boats from Turkey, Greece, Italy and Austria.

Dr. Bulic, who had charge of all the repairs and restorations of the town, who had super-intended the rebuilding of the Campanile, and had built the museum in which all the treasures had been put, was untiring in his desire to show us as much as possible. The Cathedral, dating back to the time of the ancient Greeks, almost next to which was the little chapel of the ninth century, and all the principal buildings in the town, were pointed out to us ; after which a long drive was made out to his famous villa, which was entirely built of bits of Roman remains. It was filled with treasures found in some of the excavations : statues, vases, trinkets,

s

coins and marvellous finds, all in excellent preservation.

We drank wine out of cups centuries old, and listened to tales, the like of which none of us will probably hear again.

It was with the greatest difficulty we tore ourselves away, and possibly, had we not heard in the far-off distance the warning of departure of the *Waturus*, we should have lingered even longer in this wonderful town of the Adriatic.

Zara was the last town on the Dalmatian coast at which a short halt was made; and, although the charm of this quaint old historic place was well known to us from the frequent visits we paid whilst staying at Lussin, one and all of us were delighted to roam once more across its piazza, gaze at its ancient towers and buildings, and its well-known cathedral.

We arrived at Abbazia, the Austrian Riviera, famous as a gay and fashionable resort, with its superb situation, on the edge of the Adriatic and at the foot of Monte Maggiore. Here we at once found ourselves in a totally different atmosphere.

From the terrace of the Casino, one heard strains of excellent music; and many yachts were anchored in the harbour. On the fashionable promenades one was surprised to see the same kind of brilliant, gay crowd which one is accustomed to see at Monte Carlo or Nice.

Needless to say, we were not allowed to remain long at Abbazia. After we had taken a hasty glimpse of its many charms, and had finished a festive lunch on one of the terraces of a very gay hotel, the Archduke quickly made up his mind that even a short stay amidst so much gaiety and fashion would prove irksome to the Imperial Family.

This trait in the character of a man like the Archduke, generally so gay, witty and amusing, struck one as somewhat surprising, and unlike the majority of the Viennese Court. At times he seemed to have an intense dislike to the fashionable smart world, and would seem literally to flee from it. Often and often I have known of his refusal to appear at the very last minute at some great dinner, or smart function. The guests have been announced, the dinner has been served, all have been standing waiting in the great vestibule, and the Archduke has not appeared. On the surface no surprise has been manifested, one was accustomed to wait for an

Imperial Highness, but those who guessed what had happened saw a slight frown gather on the face of Archduchess Maria Theresa. Count Chorinsky, although still wearing his imperturbable smiling mask, had found out by some mysterious means that the Archduke did not intend to be present.

A messenger would appear, "His Imperial Highness is suddenly indisposed." Most probably he *would* have taken to his bed—to read—and to avoid being hopelessly bored by a society function. Very possibly he would rise the next morning between three and four, and start off on a great hunt, miles away in the land of dense forests. He avoided as much as possible the formal receptions at a railway station; detested crowds, and all kinds of conventional and ceremonious visiting. He nearly always started before or after the rest of the Imperial Family when they were making a long train journey.

I well remember on one occasion, in the month of January, being requested to accompany Archduke Karl Stefan and the three Princes, with one of the tutors and a governess, for a cruise in Southern waters.

We left the ancient Polish château in Galicia, *en route* for the palace at Vienna; there was the usual reception, the smart officials in their resplendent uniforms, and the Court carriages from the palace. We stepped out of the train on to the crimson-carpeted platform; and, as we stood waiting for His Imperial Highness to enter the first state carriage, he turned suddenly to me and said, " Please, get in." Very much surprised, I found myself driving through the streets of Vienna in the first Court carriage with Archduke Karl and his brothers. Archduke Karl Stefan, I believe, drove through Vienna to the palace in a *fiacre*, and was perfectly happy and content.

None of us, therefore, when we were hurried from the gay and fashionable Abbazia, were in the least surprised. We all knew His Imperial Highness's horror of fashionable resorts, and smart crowds.

After so much sightseeing, Archduchess Maria Theresa then proposed three weeks' calm and quiet in Venice, and bathing in the famous Lido.

That was a great joy to all. Summer in Venice was ideal, especially in the early mornings, and late at night. Practically the whole morning was spent out on the Lido, where we were taken each time by a little steam-launch.

Once again we seemed back in the land of gaiety and fashion, for we soon found the Lido was one of those famous bathing-places where the wearing of smart costumes, head-gear, and foot-gear, is far more important than being able to swim well.

But, as the Archduke argued, we should not stay on the Lido—merely go there each day for the bathing.

There was a great terrace built out over that part of the sea where the bathing took place, and beautiful little bathing-houses were arranged along under another wide projection.

On the terrace a fine military band played morning and afternoon; gay luncheons and teas were served, and all the smart world from many European countries was to be seen daily, each trying to outdo the other in wondrous and gorgeous creations.

All the Imperial Family revelled in the bathing; the water was so warm and delicious, that an hour or more was always spent idling in the gentle waves of the beautiful Lido.

A month nearly was spent at Venice, where the nights on the Grand Canal were even more wonderful than in spring.

At last the cruise came to an end. The *Waturus* glided out of Venice, and set sail once more for Trieste, where a day or two was spent packing up, and making ready for a long train journey to Poland.

I took once more a farewell drive from Trieste, along the waters of the blue Adriatic, to the wonderful marble Palace of Miramar, which stood out at the foot of the mountains for all to see.

Marble steps led down to the edge of the water, where boats glided back with their deep orange sails. Then one looked back through a garden of tall cypress trees and gorgeous flowers, to the white marble palace beyond, which once belonged to the brother of Franz Josef, the Emperor Maximilian, who was brutally murdered in Mexico.

I wandered through the glorious rooms, filled with priceless treasures of art, and once again looked across the magnificent view of the

Adriatic and mountains beyond. A feeling of real happiness and content stole over me when I thought of the many delightful Hapsburgs I had met and known, who had given me unceasing proofs of their kindly, generous and courteous dispositions, and who had made me know the Court of Vienna as it really was.

THE END

INDEX

INDEX

267

CPSIA information can be obtained
at www.ICGtesting.com
Printed in the USA
BVHW011010230821
615013BV00003B/175